CRISTINA FERRARE'S
BIG BOWL
of LOVE

CRISTINA FERRARE'S
BIG BOWL
of LOVE

Delight Family and Friends with
More than 100 Simple, Fabulous Recipes

CRISTINA FERRARE

PHOTOGRAPHS BY
TODD PORTER AND DIANE CU

STERLING EPICURE
New York

To my sister, Diana Magaldi

STERLING EPICURE
New York

An Imprint of Sterling Publishing
387 Park Avenue South
New York, NY 10016

Book and Cover Design: Anna Christian

Food Stylists: Diane Cu and Cristina Ferrare

ISBN 978-1-4027-9830-6

Distributed in Canada by Sterling Publishing
c/o Canadian Manda Group, 165 Dufferin Street
Toronto, Ontario, Canada M6K 3H6
Distributed in the United Kingdom by GMC Distribution Services
Castle Place, 166 High Street, Lewes, East Sussex, England BN7 1XU
Distributed in Australia by Capricorn Link (Australia) Pty. Ltd.
P.O. Box 704, Windsor, NSW 2756, Australia

For information about custom editions, special sales, and premium
and corporate purchases, please contact Sterling Special Sales
at 800-805-5489 or specialsales@sterlingpublishing.com.

Manufactured in Canada

2 4 6 8 10 9 7 5 3 1

www.sterlingpublishing.com

CONTENTS

INTRODUCTION

The first publication of *Cristina Ferrare's Family Entertaining* was in the fall of 1998. Since then it has become the little cookbook that kept right on cooking! To this day people come up to me almost daily to tell me how much they enjoy preparing recipes from that book. It seems everyone can identify with the family stories and in turn tell me stories of their own families and traditions. I love it when that happens, and it makes me happy to hear that they appreciate how easy the recipes are to follow.

Food, how we shop for it, and new attitudes toward preparation and concepts have changed dramatically over the past ten years. The popularity of the Food Channel, Martha Stewart, and cooking shows in general make cooking a natural and fun thing to do—not to mention the satisfaction you get from preparing and serving home-cooked meals to your family and friends. It's like serving a *big bowl of love.*

There are numerous ways to prepare delicious, nutritious, thoughtful meals. And by thoughtful meals, I mean meals that don't intimidate, that are easy and fun to prepare, that are flavorful, exciting, and good for the soul, and that you can stretch!

Stretching the food for the meals I prepare is something I grew up with. My grandmother never threw anything away. She kept reinventing new dishes with leftovers and shopped for groceries in a way that always allowed for more meals out of the simplest ingredients. I followed her example and gave it a new twist.

I have been doing this for years. For example, out of one 5-pound chuck roast I can make three whole meals! I will show you many more ideas and demonstrate how to do exactly that with more beef, poultry, vegetables, and pastas.

I can also say, without hesitation, that in a pinch you will always have a meal that is sure to please if you keep staple items in your kitchen at all times. Even if you're too tired to go to the grocery store, you will always be able to prepare a great meal if you keep your staples on hand. I will share them with you.

Don't be intimidated by trying to prepare a great meal because you think you don't have enough time, it's too complicated or too costly, or it has too many calories. The recipes in this book are well thought out, keeping in mind that what matters is not what you eat (because I firmly believe you should never deprive yourself) but what you choose to eat and how much you eat at one time.

There is a balanced way to enjoy all the foods you love, and there are a lot of wonderful foods to choose from for happy, healthy, and at times indulgent ways of enjoying your meals! I will show you how to be able eat it all, guilt free.

Because we are all so busy, including our children, the most important thing we can do for ourselves, our families, and our friends is to use our time wisely. Connecting with one another over a meal is a great neutralizer and brings family and friends together so we can appreciate the greatest gift of all, one another.

My daughters Alexandra and Arianna have the same passion for the kitchen that I do. I am thrilled that they understand the importance of family and traditions and that they express it through their love of cooking. It's interesting to me that they have two different points of view, not on the traditions but on different approaches in preparing the same dishes that I do. It certainly leads to very interesting dynamics in the kitchen. It does get a little heated when we're all in there at the same time, and I don't mean heat from the stove. It's my turn now to sit back, hold my tongue, and not try to be right all the time. Just as I had changed my mother's and grandmother's recipes, my girls are doing the same to me. I have to admit that their remixes of the family recipes are well thought out and really, really delicious. For instance, our family Easter Sunday dinners have been pretty much the same since I was small. We always have roasted leg of lamb. My girls decided that they don't like leg of lamb anymore and instead came up with their own idea of lamb on Easter. Alex grills up baby lamb chops with a lemon salsa verde, and Arianna prepares gyros in grilled pitas with an outstanding tzatziki sauce. I have to admit, both those recipes are huge hits!

I love cooking with my daughters. It's a great bonding experience; we have a good time, and we enjoy the anticipation of "family," be it close relatives or good friends, coming to our home to share a meal.

I hope you enjoy the suggestions in this book; they represent years of experimentation to come up with ways to take the "I can't make that; it looks too hard" aspect out of preparing meals. My recipes won't intimidate, they're superdelicious, and they look pretty professional to boot! I'll share with you some secrets on how to give a "top chef" look to your dishes.

Every recipe in this book was created with the love and passion I have for cooking, my family, and my friends. Enjoy!

Love,

Cristina Ferrare

APPETIZERS

When I was a little girl, there was nothing I loved more than to sit down with family and friends and watch everyone take such delight in being together and enjoying a meal. The sounds of music in the background, clinking silver and dinnerware, and squealing children (that would be me) were so uplifting you could literally feel the love. The grown-ups enjoyed their wine while the kids sipped lemonade (no soda in our house). The great thing now, of course, is that I can enjoy great wine with my meals, just like my parents did.

Today the preparation of a meal, and its presentation and aroma, bring me back to those happy childhood memories, and it makes me happy to share my creations with my family and friends.

Whenever I serve appetizers to my guests, I serve at least two but not more than three different kinds—and I make sure not to pass out too many, so my guests won't come to the table already full. I secretly call appetizers "appespoilers" because that is what happens when you pass out too many and your guests wolf them down too fast. Just pass out enough to take the edge off and to make them excited to sit down and enjoy the meal you have so lovingly prepared.

What I love about all of these appetizers is that you can make delicious meals from the leftovers. I share these tips with you throughout the book.

TACO BITES

15 SERVINGS

Homemade tomato salsa
(page 217)

2 to 2½ cups Guacamole
(page 19)

1 tablespoon canola oil

½ pound ground chuck

2 tablespoons taco seasoning

¼ cup water

1 package mini-filo shells
(you can find them in the frozen
food section)

½ cup sharp cheddar cheese,
shredded small (I like to use
the white cheddar, but yellow is
fine too)

Leaves from 2 to 3 cilantro sprigs
for garnish

These tasty morsels are always the first to go. I have to be careful not to make too many because everyone fills up on them and then I flip out because no one is hungry for dinner!

This is a great holdover until halftime for Super Bowl Sunday or any game night!

Make the salsa. Place it in an airtight container and refrigerate.

Make the guacamole. Place the pit from the avocado in the guacamole to keep the guacamole from turning dark. Place the guacamole in an airtight container and refrigerate.

Heat a heavy skillet on medium-high heat. Add the oil and swirl it around the pan. Add the ground chuck, breaking the meat into really fine bits with a metal spatula. Brown until the beef starts to form a crust and most of the juices have evaporated.

Sprinkle 2 tablespoons of taco seasoning over the beef. Add water and cook until all the water has evaporated and the meat starts to sizzle. Keep breaking up the beef into the smallest pieces possible using the metal spatula.

Place a bowl underneath a mesh strainer and pour the beef into the strainer to strain out the excess oil. Discard the oil.

Heat the filo cups according to the package directions. Cool.

Place 1 teaspoon of the beef on the bottom of a filo cup. Spread a teaspoon of the guacamole over the beef as you would icing on a cupcake. Add 1 teaspoon of the shredded cheddar cheese, and top with a touch of the salsa. Add one small cilantro leaf on the top for garnish.

COOK'S NOTE: You can use ready-made salsa and guacamole, but I highly recommend that you take the extra time to prepare them fresh! You can even make them the day before to save time.

GUACAMOLE

4 TO 5 CUPS

We stayed with friends at their home in Acapulco for a week. The weather was steamy hot and the food was out of this world. Every night before dinner we would enjoy ice-cold slushy margaritas and the best guacamole I have ever had. Of course, I had to have the recipe and headed right into the kitchen to ask the cook. No one would give it up, not even my friend, which annoyed me to no end. So I had to resort to my secret weapon, my taste buds! I knew I would crack the case, figuring out exactly how it was made by taking the time to savor all the wonderful flavors and textures. Yes, I did it all by myself, and I have to say, I think it's spot on. Incredible guacamole, smooth, creamy, and bursting with flavor.

The secret is to start with ripe avocados; make sure they're cold. I use a potato masher and mash the heck out of the avocados until they are creamy with a bit of tiny avocado pieces still intact. A fork will do if you don't have a potato masher—it's just a little more work.

The cilantro and onion need to be chopped extremely fine, and fresh limes are a must. The recipe calls for more lime juice than I would normally use, but it really makes a difference in the taste. Warming up the tortilla chips in the oven is another must. When you dip that crunchy warm chip into the guacamole, it is a taste thrill. Bring on the shooters!

4 ripe avocados

½ medium white onion, finely chopped

½ cup cilantro, finely chopped

6 tablespoons fresh lime juice

1½ teaspoons kosher salt

2 jalapeños, 1 finely chopped, and 1 sliced thin, for garnish (optional)

1 lime, sliced thin, for garnish

Split the avocados along the sides and divide in half. Remove the pit, and scoop the avocado into a ceramic bowl. Mash with a potato masher (not a ricer) until smooth. Add the onion, cilantro, lime juice, salt, and chopped jalapeño, and continue to mash until the guacamole looks whipped and fluffy. Adjust the seasoning, adding more salt if necessary. Place an avocado pit in the middle of the guacamole to help keep it from turning dark. Garnish with sliced lime and jalapeño. Serve immediately with warm tortilla chips, or cover with plastic wrap and refrigerate until ready to serve. Refrigerate leftovers in an airtight container for up to 24 hours.

COOK'S NOTE: To warm the tortilla chips, place them on a baking sheet in the oven at 400°F for 5 to 6 minutes. Serve immediately.

STEAK BRUSCHETTA

16 SERVINGS

2 roasted red bell peppers, charred under the broiler (see page 23, Roasted Red Bell Peppers) and cut into strips

3 tablespoons olive oil

1 tablespoon chopped Italian parsley

1 tablespoon finely chopped sage

1 tablespoon finely chopped rosemary

2 garlic cloves, peeled and smashed

1 pound New York steak

1½ teaspoons kosher salt

Cracked pepper

1 Italian baguette cut on an angle into 16 (¼-inch) slices

6 ounces goat cheese

5 sprigs fresh thyme, chopped

I love these appetizers; the beef is tender and flavorful. The garlic- and olive oil–infused red bell peppers and the creamy goat cheese make a wonderful combination. Adding fresh herbs and a touch of coarse salt and cracked pepper is the perfect finishing touch. When you want to take the edge off your appetite, indulge in these. (I just want to make one huge sandwich and eat the whole thing myself!)

In a bowl combine the peppers, 1 tablespoon olive oil, parsley, sage, rosemary, and garlic. Cover and set aside.

Heat a grill pan until very hot. Sprinkle the steak with ¼ teaspoon kosher salt and cracked pepper on both sides.

Drizzle 1 tablespoon olive oil over grill pan, add beef, and grill for 10 minutes, turning every 2 minutes.

Remove the steak from the grill and let rest for 5 minutes.

Slice the steak in thin slices, and set aside.

Brush the slices of bread with 1 tablespoon olive oil on both sides, and grill for 1 minute or until grill marks show. Turn the bread over and add the goat cheese. Remove the bread from the grill.

Place the grilled bread on a serving platter, and top each slice with roasted pepper and a slice of beef. Sprinkle with finishing salt, such as fleur de sel or kosher salt, and don't forget the cracked pepper. Sprinkle on the fresh thyme.

MARINATED OLIVES

1½ CUPS

1 pound mixed olives
(purchase them already mixed,
or mix together your favorites)

1 tablespoon olive oil

2 tablespoons dried oregano

1 tablespoon thyme leaves

1 tablespoon marjoram leaves

1 teaspoon red pepper flakes

2 tablespoons lemon zest

Mixing these olives with extra-virgin olive oil and fresh herbs really brings out the flavors of these tiny mouth-watering morsels. It's extremely easy to do, and you can definitely taste the difference when you prepare the olives yourself rather than buying ready-made. Marinated olives will keep in the refrigerator in an airtight container for a month.

Drain all the brine from the olives. Place the drained olives in a bowl. Add the olive oil, oregano, thyme, marjoram, red pepper, and lemon zest. Mix well. Let stand at room temperature for 20 minutes. Mix again, and serve.

A full-bodied red wine such as cabernet sauvignon is perfect to serve with these to get the evening started!

ROASTED RED BELL PEPPERS

4 TO 6 SERVINGS

I can eat these peppers every day! I love to put them on toasted Italian or French bread, in fluffy egg-white omelets, or in panini. They can be served as a side with any meal.

Preheat the broiler to high. Place the peppers on a baking sheet. Place the baking sheet under the broiler, positioning the peppers 4 inches from the heat source. Char the peppers black on all sides, turning with tongs. Remove the peppers from the baking sheet and put them in a brown paper bag for 20 minutes to cool.

Remove the skins and seeds. Cut the peppers into strips and place in a bowl. Add olive oil, garlic, salt, pepper to taste, and parsley. Mix well. Cover with plastic wrap and place in the refrigerator for 1 hour or longer to give the garlic a chance to flavor the oil. Remove the garlic and save it for another use. Serve the peppers in a small bowl.

4 red bell peppers (if you want to throw in a yellow or orange pepper instead of using all red, that's great—mix it up!)

¼ cup olive oil

3 garlic cloves, each one cut into 4 slices

1 teaspoon kosher salt

Cracked pepper

¼ cup Italian parsley, chopped

WHITE BEAN PUREE ON GRILLED SLICED BAGUETTE

2 DOZEN OR MORE

2 cups fresh white beans, or
2 (15-ounce) cans of white beans,
drained and rinsed

¾ teaspoon kosher salt plus more
for sprinkling

Cracked pepper

1 scallion, chopped

3 tablespoons fresh lemon juice

¼ cup plus 1 tablespoon
extra-virgin olive oil

2 sprigs fresh thyme, leaves
pulled off

5 fresh basil leaves

6 lemon wedges, for garnish
(optional)

1 baguette, cut into 16 (¼-inch)
slices

Scrape the tiny herbs off
sprigs of fresh thyme
by running your fingers
down the sides of the
sprigs in the opposite
direction the thyme is
growing; they will fall
off easily.

I love beans, all kinds of beans, any way you can prepare them! I prefer to start with dried beans, and I recommend you take the time to soak them overnight. When they are cooked properly, the difference between them and the canned version is noticeable in flavor and texture. If you don't have the time to soak dried beans, though, canned beans are a great alternative; they're convenient and still packed with good-for-you protein and flavor!

Soak the fresh beans overnight, or for a quick soak bring the beans to a boil, covering the beans by 4 inches. Turn off the heat and let sit for an hour. Drain and rinse under cool water. Pour the beans back into a stockpot.

Fill a large stockpot with cool water, covering the beans by 4 inches. Do not add salt to the water, as this will make the beans tough. Bring to a boil. Turn the heat down to a gentle boil, cover, and cook until the beans are tender, usually 90 minutes for soaked beans (2 hours or more for beans that haven't been soaked). Taste test to see if the beans are tender. If they're not yet tender, cook until they are, checking every 15 minutes. Be careful to not overcook, or the beans will fall apart. If the beans have soaked up so much water while cooking that they're no longer covered by at least 4 inches of water, add more water.

Place the beans, ¾ teaspoon salt (½ teaspoon salt if using canned beans), pepper to taste, scallion, and lemon juice in a food processor. Start to slowly add the oil, and process until smooth. Adjust the seasoning, adding more salt if necessary.

Pour into a serving bowl, and drizzle 1 tablespoon of extra-virgin olive oil over the top. Sprinkle on a pinch of kosher salt, cracked pepper, and fresh chopped thyme leaves. Garnish with fresh basil and lemon wedges.

Serve with baguette slices, crostini, or crackers.

HUMMUS
WITH GRILLED PITA

2 CUPS

1 (15-ounce) can chickpeas, drained

⅔ cup extra-virgin olive oil

1 tablespoon cumin

1 garlic clove, peeled

¼ cup tahini paste

4 tablespoons fresh lemon juice

⅛ teaspoon plus a pinch of cayenne pepper

½ teaspoon kosher salt

3 pieces of pita bread, preferably the Greek kind, 8 inches across

I make hummus often because it's so easy and so good for you. Our whole family loves it, so I keep some in the refrigerator at all times. We serve it as an appetizer or for a healthy pick-me-up in the afternoon. One of my favorite ways to eat it is spread on a rice cake with a squirt of fresh lemon juice and a pinch of cayenne—a very satisfying snack.

This hummus dip goes over well on Super Bowl Sunday because of its creamy texture, nutty flavor, and spicy goodness. Besides serving it with grilled pita, pita chips, or crackers, I serve it with crudités—this way I can sneak my veggies in.

In a food processor, place the chickpeas, ⅓ cup olive oil, cumin, garlic, tahini paste, lemon juice, pepper, and salt, and process until smooth. If the mixture is too thick, add an additional 2 tablespoons olive oil and process until smooth. Brush the pita bread lightly on both sides with some of the remaining olive oil. Heat a grill pan until hot. Add the pita and grill for 30 to 40 seconds, then flip and grill the other side. Remove the pita from the grill and cut into triangles using a pizza cutter. Keep the pita slices warm in a cloth napkin.

To serve, place the hummus in a bowl with a drizzle of olive oil over the top. Sprinkle with an extra pinch of cayenne pepper, and serve with the warm pita.

TZATZIKI WITH GRILLED PITA

12 SERVINGS

My husband is Greek, so tzatziki on grilled pita is something we all love and have often! When the kids would come home from school, instead of cookies and milk I would grill up pita bread and serve this good-for-you spread made with Greek yogurt and fresh cucumbers. It's perfect with grilled lamb and as a topping for omelets.

You must use Greek-style yogurt when you make tzatziki; plain yogurt is too tart.

Most markets carry Greek-style yogurt, but if you can't find it, you can use plain yogurt; just make sure to allow enough time to prepare it: Drain plain yogurt through a cheesecloth over a bowl for at least 2 hours on your counter at room temperature. Liquid (the whey) will drip into the bowl, leaving you with a smooth yogurt that is creamy and not tart! Refrigerate the strained yogurt until you are ready to use it.

Place cucumber, olive oil, lemon juice, lemon zest, salt, mint, and dill in a bowl and mix well. Add the Greek yogurt and mix well.

Cover with plastic wrap or place in an airtight container, and chill in the refrigerator for at least 2 to 3 hours before serving.

To grill the pita bread, brush both sides with olive oil. Place on a hot grill pan or use the burner on your stovetop (watch carefully so they don't burn). Using a pizza cutter, cut the pita into quarters and serve with the tzatziki.

1 large cucumber, peeled, seeded, and diced small

1 tablespoon extra-virgin olive oil

1 tablespoon lemon juice

1 teaspoon lemon zest

1 teaspoon kosher salt

1 tablespoon fresh mint, finely chopped

¼ cup fresh dill, finely chopped

2 cups Greek yogurt

6 pieces pita bread

COOK'S NOTE: Tzatziki tastes better the day after it's made and will keep for 2 days in the refrigerator.

MARINATED ARTICHOKES

4 TO 6 SERVINGS

2 pounds frozen artichoke hearts

5 tablespoons extra-virgin olive oil

4 pieces of garlic, peeled and sliced thin

Kosher salt

1/8 teaspoon red pepper flakes

2 tablespoons fresh lemon juice

1/4 cup Italian parsley, chopped

1 lemon, sliced very thin, for garnish

Try mixing these artichoke hearts with your favorite pasta, fresh Parmesan cheese, and a squeeze of fresh lemon juice, or toss them into your favorite salad.

I have a love-hate relationship with artichokes. No matter how careful I am when I'm cleaning and preparing them, I always manage to stick myself with one of the thorns, which inevitably gets stuck in my finger, and for the life of me I can't get it out! Using the frozen kind makes me happier, and I don't have to waste time looking for the tweezers.

Cook the frozen artichoke hearts according to package directions. Drain in a colander for 10 minutes. Pat dry with a paper towel.

Heat a frying pan until hot. Add 4 tablespoons olive oil, and swirl it around the pan. Add the garlic and sauté, shaking the pan back and forth so the garlic doesn't burn. The minute the garlic starts to turn golden, quickly add the artichoke hearts. Lower the heat and continue to shake the artichokes back and forth. Add 1 teaspoon of salt and the red pepper. Using a metal spoon, stir and sauté for 8 to 10 minutes, until the artichokes start to caramelize.

Pour the artichokes into a serving bowl, add the lemon juice, and stir. Drizzle 1 tablespoon of extra-virgin olive oil over the top. Add a pinch of kosher salt, sprinkle on the parsley, and allow to cool to room temperature. Garnish with a slice of lemon.

ARTICHOKE DIP

1½ CUPS

Marinated artichokes (above)

4 ounces low-fat cream cheese

1 tablespoon lemon zest

Extra-virgin olive oil

When I make my marinated artichokes, I always double the recipe; that way, I can make this delicious dip, which I serve with crudités or crostini! Follow the recipe for marinated artichokes for this delicious, smooth, and creamy appetizer or snack.

Put the marinated artichokes and the cream cheese in a blender, and blend until creamy smooth. Pour into a bowl, add lemon zest, and mix. Drizzle a little olive oil over the top.

LAMB MEATBALLS
WITH MINT TZATZIKI

2 DOZEN MEATBALLS

Keeping a tradition from the Greek side of my family (my husband's), I thought I would give the meatball a try using spices that are synonymous with Greek cooking, such as cumin and mint. I left some spices out that traditionally go with Greek meatballs and came up with my own version and paired it with the traditional sauce called tzatziki, which I love. The results were fantastic—a big hit. Tony and my girls love it.

In the bowl with the lamb, add onion, garlic, egg, bread crumbs, cumin, mayonnaise, fresh mint, and salt. Using your hands, mix thoroughly to distribute the ingredients evenly. With a teaspoon, form the mixture into 24 meatballs. Don't level the meat off or pack the meatballs too tightly.

Preheat the broiler.

Lightly spread canola oil on a baking sheet using a paper towel. Place the meatballs 2 inches apart on the baking sheet, and position the baking sheet 4 inches from the heat source. Broil for about 5 minutes, turning once halfway through.

Arrange the meatballs on a serving platter, and squeeze fresh lemon juice over the top. Sprinkle the cayenne pepper over the meatballs at the last minute. Serve at once with mint tzatziki (page 27).

1 pound ground lamb

3 tablespoons red onion, finely chopped

1 small garlic clove, minced or crushed in a garlic press

1 egg, slightly beaten

2 tablespoons bread crumbs

1 teaspoon cumin

1 tablespoon mayonnaise

1 cup fresh mint, loosely packed and finely chopped

¾ teaspoon kosher salt

2 tablespoons canola oil

1 fresh lemon for squeezing and garnish, cut into quarters

⅛ teaspoon cayenne pepper, optional

ANTIPASTO PLATTER

8 TO 10 SERVINGS

2 loaves Italian or French bread

Extra-virgin olive oil

20 slices sopressata or Genoa salami

20 slices mortadella

20 slices prosciutto

6 ounces (approximately 1½ cups) Parmesan cheese, cut into chunks

1 cup marinated artichokes (page 28)

1 cup marinated olives (page 22)

1 cup white bean puree (page 24)

3 roasted red bell peppers (page 23)

When I was growing up, Sunday and holiday dinners always started with a huge platter of antipasto. I loved to arrange the platters and made sure to create a masterpiece, because even as a child I believed people ate with their eyes. The only problem was that everything looked so delicious that I would always eat way too many of the appetizers, and then when it came time to have dinner I was so full I couldn't eat another bite!

To prepare the crostini, adjust the oven rack to the middle position. Preheat the oven to 400°F.

Cut the bread on an angle into ¼-inch-thick slices. Brush both sides of each slice lightly with olive oil and place on a baking sheet. Bake until the bread turns golden and crispy, approximately 15 to 20 minutes. (There's no need to turn the slices over halfway through.) You should have more than two dozen slices. You can make the crostini up to four days before you use them; store them in an airtight container.

Arrange the salami, mortadella, prosciutto, and Parmesan cheese on a large platter without overcrowding. Serve the crostini, artichokes, olives, white bean puree, and peppers alongside in separate bowls.

COOK'S NOTE: Use the leftover marinated artichokes, roasted peppers, and Parmesan cheese as a topping for a pizza. Sprinkle on red chili flakes, a drizzle of olive oil, bake, and you have yourself one mean pizza! You can also turn the marinated artichokes into a dip (page 28).

Save any leftover crostini to use for bread crumbs. Place in a food processor and process until you have small, coarsely chopped bread crumbs.

SALADS

I feel very fortunate to live in California, where I have access to fresh produce all the time. My favorite thing to do is to shop for the freshest seasonal fruits and vegetables at the open market every Wednesday and Sunday. In fact, I keep a rolling collapsible cart in the trunk of my car just in case I happen to spot an open market when I'm traveling. I just love walking up and down the aisles to check out what the vendors have available, then picking out delicious treasures to take home. The heady smell of the freshly picked organic fruits and vegetables permeates the aisles; their earthy aroma makes my head spin. I love that smell! Speaking of organic, I only buy organic. Yes, it is more expensive, but the difference in the flavor is dramatic. More important, I am a believer in trying to avoid ingesting pesticides.

I eat at least two salads every day, and I always serve a salad with meals. There are many ways to prepare a bowl of salad using different kinds of greens; wild baby arugula is one of my favorites. Long gone are the salads made with iceberg lettuce, sliced or quartered tomatoes, and peeled sliced cucumbers with ranch dressing.

One of my favorite meals is a hearty bowl of soup followed by a fresh crisp salad filled with earthly delights—a rewarding end to a perfect (or not-so-perfect) day!

ROASTED BEET AND ARUGULA SALAD WITH BALSAMIC SYRUP

6 SERVINGS

½ cup pignoli nuts

8 teaspoons extra-virgin olive oil

4 pounds mixed beets, red and gold, scrubbed

6 cups baby or wild arugula, washed and dried

½ teaspoon kosher salt

4 tablespoons Shallot Vinaigrette (page 200)

6 ounces goat cheese, rolled into 30 balls the size of small grapes

6 teaspoons Reduced Balsamic Syrup (page 206)

I never liked beets; I always thought they tasted like dirt, and I just couldn't swallow them. A friend of mine managed to talk me into tasting a beet that had been roasted in the oven instead of boiled—and I loved it. There's something about roasting that brings out the beet's natural sugar and pleasant earthy-sweet taste. Adding arugula, goat cheese, and balsamic syrup gives the dish a bite and the old-fashioned beet a contemporary new look and taste.

I'm a convert now. My family loves this dish, and I serve it all year round.

Place the pignoli nuts in a small dry frying pan and turn the stove to medium-high heat. Shake the pan back and forth until the pine nuts have started to turn golden, approximately 5 minutes. Remove from heat and set aside.

Pour 2 teaspoons of olive oil in the palm of your hand and rub the beets all over to coat. Place the beets on a baking dish whole, and bake for 1 hour and 15 minutes, or until tender. To check for doneness, insert a sharp paring knife through the middle of the thickest part of the beet. If the knife goes through all the way smoothly, the beets are done. Remove from the oven and cool completely.

Peel the beets under running water and cut them into thin slices. Arrange 6 slices of beets on a salad plate in a circle, alternating the colors.

Toss the arugula with kosher salt and dressing. Place 1 cup of arugula on top of the beets. Spread 4 to 5 goat-cheese balls around the salad, and top with 2 teaspoons of pignoli nuts. Drizzle 1 teaspoon of balsamic syrup and 1 teaspoon of olive oil over each serving.

Repeat the assembly procedure for the other 5 servings.

TOMATO-MOZZARELLA TOWER WITH SHALLOT-BACON DRESSING

6 SERVINGS

6 slices really good white bread, not the soft stuff

12 baby Roma tomatoes, red and yellow, for garnish (optional)

6 slices bacon

2 tablespoons finely chopped shallots

2 tablespoons apple cider vinegar

6 heirloom tomatoes; make sure the tomatoes are uniform in size (if you can't find heirlooms, use regular tomatoes)

2 (6-ounce) packages buffalo mozzarella

10 fresh basil leaves

Kosher salt

Cracked pepper

1 to 2 tablespoons Reduced Balsamic Syrup (page 206)

When I want to impress my family and friends, I make these tomato towers. They taste like a BLT. I make this dish often during the summer months, too, when tomatoes are at their peak flavor.

This dish has a lot going on. You have the sweetness of the tomatoes and the creamy goodness of the mozzarella cheese. Then there are the crunchy, salty bits of bacon and the smoky flavor of the shallot dressing, along with the grilled bread. When you top it off with fresh basil and thick balsamic syrup and take your first bite, it's like a circus in your mouth!

It's important to have all your ingredients ready before you start to assemble your tower.

Cut 6 bread rounds using a 4½-inch cookie cutter. Set aside.

Slice the baby Roma tomatoes in half lengthwise. Set aside.

Fry the bacon in a skillet until crispy. Remove the bacon from the skillet and place on a paper towel to absorb excess oil. Lower the heat under the skillet to medium, add the shallots to the bacon drippings, and sauté for 30 seconds, until the shallots start to turn a bit crispy.

Add the apple cider vinegar, and with a wooden spoon, stir well, scraping the brown bits from the bottom of the pan. Pour into a small bowl and set aside to use as dressing.

Return the skillet to the stove over medium heat. Add as many bread rounds as will fit in the pan. Lightly toast both sides of the bread. Be careful that the flame isn't too high; you don't want to burn the bread, so stay with it until all 6 pieces have been toasted lightly. Set aside.

Crumble the cooked bacon into small bits and set aside in a small bowl.

Cut the heirloom tomatoes into slices slightly less than ½ inch thick. You should have 18 slices that are consistent in size. You will have some tomato left over.

Cut the buffalo mozzarella into slices slightly less than ½ inch thick. You should have 12 slices that are consistent in size.

Stack all 10 of the basil leaves on top of one another, roll them into a cigarette shape, and slice thin.

Make an assembly line: toasted bread, heirloom tomatoes, sliced mozzarella, shallot dressing, bacon bits, kosher salt, basil, balsamic syrup.

Place one toasted bread round on a salad plate, add a slice of heirloom tomato, and sprinkle with a small pinch each of salt and pepper.

Drizzle on several drops of shallot dressing and a pinch of crumbled bacon, letting a little fall onto the plate as well.

Top with a slice of mozzarella cheese and then another slice of tomato.

Repeat this process until you have three slices of heirloom tomato and two slices of mozzarella cheese in your tower.

On the last tomato slice, the one that tops the tower, sprinkle more bacon bits, then lightly drizzle more dressing (a little goes a long way), including some on the plate for a professional look. Garnish with a few strips of basil and balsamic syrup.

Add 5 to 6 baby Roma tomato halves to the plate and sprinkle with a pinch of kosher salt, if you like.

Repeat the assembly process for the other 5 towers.

LIGHT CAESAR SALAD

10 SERVINGS

Most Caesar salads are dripping with thick, creamy, or oily dressings that weigh down the salad and add extra calories. There are only 4 tablespoons of dressing in this salad, though, and the dressing is light and doesn't have a heavy aftertaste.

Make the croutons first. Place the oven rack in the middle position. Preheat the oven to 350°F.

Add the smashed garlic clove to the olive oil and let sit for 20 minutes to infuse the oil with the garlic flavor.

Place the bread cubes in a bowl. Remove the garlic from the oil, pour the oil over the bread cubes, and toss to coat. Spread the bread cubes in an even layer on a baking sheet, and bake for 15 to 20 minutes or until golden and crunchy. Stir occasionally while baking to make sure they don't burn. Cool on the baking sheet until they reach room temperature.

Remove the large outer leaves from the heads of lettuce and discard. Wash the rest of the leaves, dry them well, and tear them into 1½-inch pieces (about 9 or 10 cups).

To make the dressing, in a medium glass bowl combine the lemon juice, mustard, Worcestershire sauce, salt, garlic, and anchovy paste, and whisk until smooth. Combine the olive oil and canola oil, and whisk together for a few seconds. Whisking constantly, add the oil in a slow, steady stream to the anchovy mixture.

To assemble the salad, place the lettuce in a salad bowl. Add 4 tablespoons of dressing, and toss, distributing evenly. Add ½ cup freshly grated Parmesan cheese and toss again. Add the croutons and anchovies (if you are using them) and toss. Sprinkle on 2 tablespoons of Parmesan cheese and a handful of extra croutons. The croutons can be stored in an airtight container for up to 1 week. You can also use them to make bread crumbs.

Garlic-infused croutons

1 garlic clove, peeled and smashed

3 tablespoons extra-virgin olive oil

3 cups ½-inch bread cubes from 1 baguette or sourdough loaf

Salad and Caesar dressing

2 heads romaine lettuce

1 tablespoon plus 2 teaspoons fresh lemon juice

1 teaspoon Dijon mustard

1 teaspoon Worcestershire sauce

¼ teaspoon kosher salt

1 small to medium garlic clove, minced or pressed through a garlic press

4 anchovy fillets, chopped into a paste

¼ cup extra-virgin olive oil

2 tablespoons canola oil

½ cup plus 2 tablespoons freshly grated Parmesan cheese

1 small can anchovies, for garnish

COOK'S NOTE: You will have more than enough dressing—at least 4 tablespoons extra, which is enough for another salad. The dressing will keep in the refrigerator for 24 hours. Shake well before using.

CUCUMBER AND ZUCCHINI CARPACCIO SALAD

4 TO 6 SERVINGS

¼ cup extra-virgin olive oil

4 tablespoons fresh lemon juice

1 tablespoon rice wine vinegar

1 tablespoon finely chopped fresh mint

2 teaspoons finely chopped fresh dill

1 tablespoon finely chopped Italian parsley

2 zucchini, sliced paper-thin

2 cucumbers, sliced paper-thin

½ teaspoon kosher salt

½ cup feta cheese, crumbled

¼ cup finely chopped roasted walnuts

Freshly cracked pepper

In the summer, when there is an overabundance of cucumbers and zucchini and fresh herbs, I make this salad often. It's light and full of fresh flavor; it's also very beautiful to look at when presented this way.

In a glass bowl, whisk together the olive oil, lemon juice, vinegar, mint, dill, and parsley. Set aside.

Slice the vegetables on a mandolin or a vegetable slicer that can slice paper-thin. Arrange the zucchini and cucumbers alternately on a large platter. Sprinkle lightly all over with kosher salt. Drizzle 3 tablespoons of the vinaigrette over the top, add the crumbled feta, and sprinkle with walnuts and cracked pepper to taste. If you are not going to use the salad right away, do not add the vinaigrette; instead, cover with plastic wrap and refrigerate until you are ready to serve.

NONTRADITIONAL GREEK SALAD WITH CHICKEN CROQUETTES

6 TO 8 SERVINGS

Here's a different twist on the classic Greek salad—with an added surprise. I took some liberties here, and I know I'll hear about it from the Greek side of my family. Maybe I shouldn't mess with the tried and true, but I wanted an alternative to the traditional Greek salad. I've kept all the lovely flavors, but I substituted tender baby greens for the romaine lettuce. I cut the vegetables into smaller pieces and added a lot of fresh herbs, and as an added bonus I included chicken croquettes stuffed with feta cheese on the side. I tried this dish on my Greek husband, and he really loved it—whew! Now I just have to get by the family back east.

To make the dressing, in a bowl whisk together olive oil, shallot, onion, vinegars, and lemon juice. Set aside.

Make the croquettes, and keep them covered with foil until you're ready to serve.

To assemble the salad, put the greens into a wooden salad bowl. Add the celery, diced and sliced cucumbers, bell pepper, onion, mint, parsley, and oregano leaves.

Sprinkle salt on top of the greens, and drizzle on 5 tablespoons of dressing. Toss well.

Top the salad with chunks of feta cheese and olives. Add kosher salt and cracked pepper to taste.

Serve on salad plates with a chicken croquette on the side of each plate. Add a lemon wedge to squirt on the croquette. Opa!

Dressing

½ cup extra-virgin olive oil

1 tablespoon medium shallot, minced

1 tablespoon finely chopped red onion

1 tablespoon apple cider vinegar

2 ½ tablespoons rice wine vinegar

1 tablespoon fresh lemon juice

Croquettes and salad

8 chicken croquettes (page 104)

½ pound mixed baby greens, rinsed and dried in a salad spinner, and chilled in the refrigerator for 30 minutes

2 celery ribs, cut at an angle into bite-size chunks

2 cucumbers, 1½ peeled, seeded, and diced, ½ cut into slices with skins on

1 red bell pepper, seeds removed and sliced thin

5 thin slices of red onion

10 sprigs of fresh mint, chopped coarsely

10 sprigs of Italian parsley, chopped coarsely

Leaves from 6 sprigs of fresh oregano

¼ teaspoon salt

2 cups Greek feta cut into chunks

16 Greek olives

Kosher salt

Cracked pepper

8 lemon wedges for garnish

BUTTER LETTUCE WITH FETA, WALNUTS, AND OLIVE OIL AND LEMON DRESSING

4 TO 6 SERVINGS

½ cup walnuts, chopped

2 heads butter lettuce, rinsed and spun dry (place back in the refrigerator to keep the leaves cold)

Kosher salt

⅓ cup Shallot Vinaigrette (page 200) plus additional if desired

1 cup feta cheese, crumbled

Pomegranate seeds to sprinkle on top of the salad (if pomegranates are not in season, you can use dried cranberries or cherries)

2 tablespoons finely chopped Italian parsley

This is a beautiful and delicate salad that I usually serve after the main course; it's a lovely way to finish a great meal.

Handle the leaves delicately while you rinse them in cool water. Use a salad spinner to spin the leaves dry, and make sure to get as much water as you can off the leaves. Too much water left on the leaves will make the salad taste flat because the dressing won't adhere to the leaves properly. It helps if you place the butter lettuce back into the refrigerator after you spin it dry. Chilling the leaves for about 15 minutes helps to retain their texture.

Toast the walnuts by placing them in a small dry frying pan. Turn the heat to medium, and toss and shake the nuts back and forth until they have browned and released their fragrant oils, about 4 to 5 minutes. You will be able to smell the aroma. Be careful not to burn the walnuts; they will end up tasting rancid. Place in a small bowl and set aside.

Place the butter lettuce in a salad bowl.

Sprinkle salt over the lettuce. Pour 5 tablespoons of the dressing over the lettuce, and gently toss. If you feel the salad is too dry and needs more dressing, add 1 tablespoon at a time.

Evenly distribute the lettuce among 6 to 8 plates. Garnish with feta cheese, pomegranate seeds, parsley, and walnuts.

Serve with a piece of crusty sourdough baguette that you have warmed in a 350°F oven for 5 minutes.

COOK'S NOTE: Goat cheese goes nicely with this salad too, if you prefer it instead of feta.

CHICKEN TOSTADA SALAD

6 SERVINGS

I love to make this salad with leftover chicken (or substitute grilled sliced beef, shrimp, or turkey). It's so easy to do, and with my staple and pantry items (page 219), I can make this dish anytime.

I eliminate extra calories with this recipe, without compromising great flavor, by using low-fat whole wheat tortillas. Instead of frying them in oil, I bake them in the oven until they are crispy and crunchy.

If you want to make your own salsa, you can make it the day before (although store-bought salsa and guacamole are perfectly good). It will keep in the refrigerator in an airtight container for 3 to 4 days.

Preheat the oven to 400°F. Spray the tortillas on both sides with cooking spray. Place them in the oven on the rack and bake for 20 to 30 minutes, until crisp and golden brown. Keep an eye on them so they don't burn. Remove from the oven and set aside.

To make the lemon dressing, in a glass bowl combine the olive oil, lemon juice, vinegar, and kosher salt, and mix well. Set aside.

Make the tomato salsa and guacamole if you are not using store-bought. Cover and set aside in the refrigerator.

To make the bean salsa, in a bowl, combine the beans, red and yellow peppers, celery, scallions, jalapeño, olive oil, lemon juice, cumin, salt, pepper to taste, and cilantro. Mix well. If you have the time, cover and let sit in the refrigerator for an hour; it will bring out the many layers of flavors. Any leftovers will keep in the refrigerator for 2 days.

When you are ready to serve, drizzle 3 tablespoons of lemon dressing over the arugula or baby greens and mix well. Place one tortilla on each plate. Spread 2 tablespoons of guacamole over each tortilla. Add ½ cup of bean salsa toward the middle of the tortilla. Add 1 cup of arugula or greens over the bean salsa. Top with ½ cup chopped chicken, as much of the tomato salsa as you like, and 2 tablespoons of Monterey jack (more if desired). Garnish with fresh cilantro sprigs and diced jalapeño. Serve with lime wedges.

Lemon dressing

¼ cup extra-virgin olive oil

3 tablespoons fresh lemon juice

1 tablespoon rice wine vinegar

¼ teaspoon kosher salt

Bean salsa

2 (15-ounce) cans black beans, drained and rinsed

1 medium red bell pepper, diced small

1 medium yellow bell pepper, diced small

2 celery ribs, diced small

2 scallions, chopped small

1 tablespoon diced jalapeño

2 tablespoons extra-virgin olive oil

2 tablespoons fresh lemon juice

1 teaspoon cumin

½ teaspoon kosher salt

Cracked pepper

2 tablespoons chopped cilantro

Assembly

6 (8-inch) whole wheat tortillas

2 cups Tomato Salsa (page 217)

2 cups Guacamole (page 19)

6 cups wild arugula or baby greens

3 cups chopped roasted chicken breast (1½-inch pieces)

1½ cups shredded Monterey jack cheese

8 fresh cilantro sprigs

1 small jalapeño, seeded and diced

6 lime wedges

SOUPS

I keep fresh chicken stock in my refrigerator at all times. I use it in so many of my recipes—from dishes made with chicken and beef to sauces and gravies. Whenever I'm looking for a quick meal that's satisfying and easy too, I pull out my supply of stock from the fridge or pantry and whip up one of my recipes for a delicious bowl of goodness.

There is nothing I enjoy better than sitting down to a hearty serving of piping-hot soup. In fact, I like to start my meals with a serving of soup, hot or cold. Many nights, actually, I have what I call "a meal in a bowl" because everything I love is in one delicious bowl—hearty vegetables, chicken, shrimp, or beef, beans, and pasta or rice!

Practically everything in my refrigerator ends up, sooner or later, in a pot of soup. I *never* throw away vegetables, no matter how old or sad they may get; I just make them into a fantastic bowl of soup before they turn the corner and have to be tossed. You know the ones I'm talking about, the carrots that bend slightly and the celery that has just begun to lose its crispy crunch, the broccoli that has seen better days, the squash that is starting to look squashed, and the onions that are starting to sprout new leaves. Save them; don't toss them. You can turn them into creamy, velvety soups; there are recipes in this chapter for soups like that using carrots and butternut squash that will surprise you. Of course, I try to never get to the point of having to use veggies that have lost their spark, but sometimes you have to be creative so you don't waste anything!

ROASTED CHICKEN STOCK

1 (4- to 5-pound) roasted chicken, homemade or store-bought

2 medium-size onions, cut in half, skin on

4 medium carrots, peeled and chopped in quarters

6 pieces of celery, tops on, cut in quarters

½ bunch of Italian parsley, rinsed

3 garlic cloves, skin on, smashed

1 tablespoon table salt

4 slices fresh lemon

4 to 5 black peppercorns

3 quarts water

I never throw out chicken bones. If I'm too lazy to make the stock right away or don't have the time, I just put the bones in a plastic bag and pop it in the freezer until I'm ready. I also freeze chicken stock in ice cube trays. I use blocks of frozen stock when I'm making sauces or gravy, or deglazing a pan.

There isn't a better way to stretch your meals than by using a simple roasted chicken. I always have chicken stock in my refrigerator. It's a lifesaver because I know I can always use it to come up with something fantastic, even in an emergency. There are so many ways to convert a simple stock into great meals.

To be perfectly honest, I often use the prepared roasted chickens from the grocery store to make chicken stock. I prefer to use the bones from a roasted chicken because the stock turns out heartier. Using store-bought is also convenient, and saves time and money. I can bring two chickens home and know that I can use them to make at least five great meals and freeze them. The many recipe suggestions in this book will help you do so too.

Enjoy!

Remove the meat from the bones of the roasted chicken. Place the meat in a bowl, cover, and refrigerate.

In a large stockpot combine the chicken bones, onions, carrots, celery, parsley, garlic, salt, lemon slices, and peppercorns. Add 3 quarts of water. On high heat bring the soup to a boil; then turn the heat down to a gentle simmer. Cover the pot and simmer for 1 hour.

Pour the soup through a colander into a large pot to separate the broth from the bones and vegetables; discard the bones and vegetables. If you are going to put the stock in the fridge instead of using it right away, make sure you cool it to room temperature before you do. Pour the cooled stock into a container, cover, and refrigerate. It will last for a week in the refrigerator and up to 3 months in the freezer. If you have refrigerated the stock overnight, you will notice that all of the fat has risen to the top. Simply skim it off the top and discard.

REVISED ITALIAN WEDDING SOUP

6 TO 8 SERVINGS

When I was a little girl, my mother and grandmother would make a soup that I just didn't like at all. It was a traditional soup called Italian wedding soup, with little beef meatballs and spinach. I so disliked it, I swore I was never going to get married because I thought I would have to eat it on my wedding day. I have since revised the recipe and taken some liberties, and now I can't get enough. And yes, I would serve it at my wedding if I were to marry my Tony again!

Make the chicken stock first.

Preheat the oven to 350°F.

Combine the ground chicken, sausage, bread crumbs, Parmesan and Romano cheese, parsley, milk, and egg in a bowl. Mix well.

Line a baking pan with parchment paper. Using a teaspoon, drop meatballs onto the baking pan, spaced about 2 inches apart. Bake for 30 minutes, until lightly browned.

Cook the pasta according to the package directions, drain, rinse, and set aside.

Bring the chicken stock to a gentle boil. Add the cooked pasta. Add the meatballs, and simmer for 1 minute. Add the spinach and bring back up to a gentle boil. Cook for 1 minute. Taste for enough salt, and adjust the seasoning.

Ladle into warm bowls, sprinkle on plenty of Parmesan cheese, and garnish with chives.

Meatballs

¾ pound ground chicken

2 mild Italian sausages, casings removed

½ cup plain bread crumbs

¼ cup Parmesan cheese, plus additional to sprinkle over the soup

¼ cup Pecorino Romano cheese

2 tablespoons chopped fresh Italian parsley

3 tablespoons whole milk

1 egg, slightly beaten

Soup

8 ounces small pasta (small tube pasta, baby bow ties, or small shells)

4 quarts Roasted Chicken Stock (page 52) or store-bought organic chicken broth

3 cups baby spinach

16 chives

CHICKEN SOUP WITH CHICKEN MEATBALLS AND PASTINA

8 TO 10 SERVINGS

3 quarts Roasted Chicken Stock (page 52)

Approximately 2 cups of cut-up cooked chicken (you can use the chicken you put aside when you made the stock)

1 egg yolk

2 scallions, minced

1 tablespoon minced Italian parsley

¼ cup freshly grated Parmesan cheese

¼ cup Romano cheese

½ teaspoon kosher salt

Cracked pepper

1 cup uncooked pastina, orzo, or any small pasta

2 tablespoons finely chopped chives or parsley (or both)

I could always tell when my kids weren't feeling well. The first thing they would say to me before they told me their throat hurt was, "Mom, would you make me some chicken soup with pastina?" To this day, even though they are adults, when they're not feeling well they ask me if I would make chicken soup with pastina and bring it to them. Of course, I can't get there fast enough.

But you don't have to have a fever to enjoy this soup. I make it all the time and serve it to company as well. It's a conversation starter, too; guests look down at their bowl of piping-hot soup and ask, "What are those little things in the soup that look like stars?"

When you grow up in an Italian household, pastina is a must. It is one of the very first foods we were given as babies: teeny, tiny bits of pasta that my grandmother used to say were *piccole stelle dal cielo*—little stars from heaven.

Make the chicken stock first.

In a food processor, combine the chicken, egg yolk, scallions, parsley, Parmesan and Romano cheese, salt, and pepper to taste. Process until the chicken pieces are small. Finish mixing everything together with a spatula. Do not overprocess, and do not overmix. Shape the mixture into tiny meatballs about the size of a large purple grape. Set aside.

Cook pastina or desired small pasta according to package directions, drain, rinse, and set aside.

Meanwhile, bring the chicken broth to a gentle boil; then bring to a simmer and add meatballs (boiling will break up the meatballs). Cook for 10 minutes.

Add the cooked pastina, and heat through until hot. Taste and adjust seasoning as needed.

Sprinkle chopped chives and cracked pepper on top. Serve piping hot.

CHICKEN SOUP WITH TORTELLINI FILLING IN WONTON WRAPPERS

6 TO 8 SERVINGS

I was taught as a little girl how to make pasta dough. It's fun, but who has the time anymore? Now you can buy fresh pasta dough at the market, and using ready-made wonton squares is a lifesaver! They're so easy to work with, and whatever you fill them with always turns out light and delicate!

Make the chicken stock first.

In a food processor, combine ¾ cup of diced roasted chicken, the mortadella, egg, nutmeg, and cheese. Process until smooth.

Spray a cookie sheet with cooking spray to lay your filled wontons on.

Lay out 18 wonton wrappers on the counter. Place 1 heaping teaspoon of the chicken mixture in the middle of a wrapper. Dip both of your index fingers in water, and run them along all four sides of the wonton wrapper to moisten. Fold the wrapper in half on the diagonal, pressing the sides together to create a triangle. Bring the two corners nearest the fold together in the back, and press them together firmly.

Place the wonton on the cookie sheet. Repeat this process until all of the wontons are complete.

Bring the soup to a gentle boil, and add the soy sauce. Add the wontons and the remaining diced chicken. Simmer for 10 minutes.

Ladle the hot soup into warm bowls, putting two wontons into each bowl. Sprinkle with scallions and chopped parsley.

3½ quarts Roasted Chicken Stock (page 52) or store-bought organic chicken broth

3 cups diced roasted chicken

3 slices mortadella, chopped

1 egg, slightly beaten

½ teaspoon grated nutmeg

½ cup grated Parmesan cheese

1 (12-ounce) package of wonton wrappers

1 small bowl water

⅓ cup low-sodium soy sauce

2 scallions, finely chopped

1 tablespoon finely chopped Italian parsley

COOK'S NOTE: Each 12-ounce package of wontons contains 60 wrappers; you will need 36 for this recipe. Wrap the leftover wonton wrappers tightly in plastic wrap, and store in the refrigerator for up to 1 week.

AVGOLEMONO SOUP WITH ORZO

6 SERVINGS

2 quarts Roasted Chicken Stock (page 52) or store-bought organic chicken broth

1½ cups uncooked orzo

4 egg yolks, lightly beaten

3 tablespoons fresh lemon juice

1 tablespoon lemon zest

1 cup diced chicken breast, covered and set aside in the refrigerator until ready to use (you can use the chicken you put aside when you made the stock, any leftover chicken you have on hand, or chicken pieces from the deli)

Kosher salt

Pepper

2 tablespoons finely chopped Italian parsley

2 fresh lemons, thinly sliced (12 slices)

My husband is Greek, so I make this soup often for my family and dinner guests. Since I always have chicken stock in the fridge or in my pantry, eggs and roasted chicken in the fridge, fresh lemons in my fruit bowl, and orzo in my pantry, I can conjure up this soup anytime. It's full of flavor, and the tang from the fresh lemons gives this soup its distinctive flavor.

Make the chicken stock first.

In a large saucepan, bring 5 cups of water plus 1 teaspoon of salt to a boil. Add the orzo and mix. Cook until soft, drain, rinse, and set aside.

In a stockpot, bring the chicken stock to a boil; turn down the heat to medium.

To temper the egg yolks, add a ladleful of the hot chicken stock into the bowl with the egg yolks while constantly whisking to prevent the yolks from curdling. Add lemon juice and lemon zest.

Reduce the heat under the stock to low. Using a whisk, slowly add in the tempered eggs. When all the yolks have been whisked in, use a wooden spoon and stir constantly until the soup is slightly thickened, 4 to 5 minutes.

Add the cooked orzo and diced chicken, and mix. Do not let the soup boil again, because it will promote curdling, and you want the soup to have a thick, creamy consistency. Simmer gently on low heat for 1 to 2 minutes, until the chicken is heated through. Adjust the seasoning, adding salt and pepper if necessary.

Ladle the soup into warm bowls, and garnish with parsley and 2 thin slices of lemon. Serve immediately.

ROASTED BUTTERNUT SQUASH SOUP

4 TO 6 SERVINGS

Butternut squash makes a creamy, satisfying bowl of comfort.
I caramelize the onions to help bring out the natural nutty taste of
the squash. You've probably noticed by now that I use low-fat or nonfat
cream cheese in a lot of my vegetable soup recipes. That's because
the cream cheese helps with the consistency and adds a deeper, richer,
fuller flavor to soup.

Preheat the oven 325°F.

In a rimmed baking sheet, spread out the sliced onions and add 1
tablespoon of olive oil and 1 teaspoon of kosher salt. Set aside.

Place the squash in a roasting pan, drizzle 1 tablespoon of olive oil over
the top, and use your hands to rub the oil all over the squash to coat.

Place the tray with the squash and the tray with the onions in the oven.
Roast the onions for 45 minutes or until the onions have caramelized
and are mostly a deep golden brown. Remove from oven and set aside.

Roast the squash for 1 hour or until you can insert a paring knife through
the middle easily. Remove from the oven and let cool for 30 minutes.

Slice the squash in half, scoop out and discard the seeds, and scrape
out the flesh and place it in a stockpot. Add the caramelized onions,
cinnamon, cloves, nutmeg, scallions, chicken stock, and sherry. Simmer
gently for 30 minutes.

In a blender, in batches, add 2 ladlefuls of soup and 2 ounces of the
cream cheese at a time, and blend until smooth, for 1 minute. Pour into
a clean stockpot. Continue this process until all of the soup and all of the
cream cheese is used. Taste and adjust seasoning as needed.

To serve, heat the soup until hot but not boiling, and ladle into heated
bowls. Garnish each bowl with 1 tablespoon sour cream, ½ teaspoon
chopped scallions, a pinch of finely chopped jalapeños, and a dash of
cayenne pepper. A drizzle of truffle oil will put this over the top. If you
don't want to use truffle oil, try olive oil or walnut oil.

2 medium onions, peeled and
sliced

2 tablespoons extra-virgin olive oil

1 teaspoon kosher salt

3 pounds butternut squash

½ teaspoon ground cinnamon

Pinch of ground cloves

¼ teaspoon grated nutmeg

5 scallions, chopped

2 quarts chicken stock, homemade
(page 52), or store-bought organic
chicken broth

2 teaspoons dry sherry or dry
white wine

8 ounces nonfat or low-fat cream
cheese, room temperature and
cut into pieces

6 to 8 tablespoons sour cream

3 teaspoons chopped scallions

1 ½ teaspoons diced jalapeños,
for garnish

Cayenne pepper

½ teaspoon truffle oil, extra-virgin
olive oil, or walnut oil

PUMPKIN SOUP

6 TO 8 SERVINGS

Soup

⅓ cup olive oil

2 medium onions, thinly sliced

4 scallions, chopped

1 tablespoon dry sherry

1 teaspoon ground cinnamon

⅛ teaspoon ground cloves

1 teaspoon freshly grated nutmeg

1½ teaspoons kosher salt

Pinch of cayenne pepper

1 (29-ounce) can pure pumpkin

1 quart homemade chicken stock (page 52) or store-bought organic chicken broth

1 (8-ounce) package low-fat cream cheese, cut into small pieces

Garnish

6 to 8 tablespoons low-fat or nonfat sour cream (1 tablespoon per serving)

4 scallions, finely chopped

1 small jalapeño, sliced thin (optional)

¼ cup pomegranate seeds

Walnut oil or olive oil for drizzling (optional)

¼ cup toasted pumpkin seeds

This is the perfect cold-weather soup, hot and creamy, without the calories! It's one of my very favorite soups to serve all winter long. On Thanksgiving I offer it to my family and guests when they first arrive. I serve it in a demitasse cup or small coffee cup or teacup. It gives everyone something warm and satisfying to whet their appetites while waiting for the big meal.

On medium-high heat, heat a saucepan or stockpot until hot. Add the olive oil; then quickly add the onions and scallions and stir. Turn heat down to medium. Sauté until the onions start to caramelize (about 10 to 12 minutes). Add sherry and stir. Add the cinnamon, cloves, nutmeg, salt, cayenne pepper, and pumpkin, and mix well. Add the chicken stock and stir until all of the ingredients have blended together well. Lower the heat and simmer for 20 minutes, until the soup starts to thicken slightly. If the soup is too thick, add more chicken stock or water, ½ cup at a time. Turn off heat.

Fill a blender halfway with the soup and half of the cream cheese. Blend until smooth. Pour into a soup pot. Continue the process with the rest of the soup and the cream cheese until everything has been blended.

Place the soup pot back on the stove and heat through.

Serve soup piping hot, garnished with a dollop of sour cream, finely chopped scallions, chopped jalapeño, pomegranate seeds, a drizzle of walnut or olive oil, and pumpkin seeds.

COOK'S NOTE: To toast the pumpkin seeds, place ¼ cup seeds in a small dry frying pan and heat until the seeds start to brown. They will release their oils and a lovely aroma.

BACON, LETTUCE, AND TOMATO SOUP

4 SERVINGS

I came up with this soup one night when I craved a BLT sandwich. It was freezing cold that night and I wanted something warm and soothing. I thought if I combined my favorite sandwich ever with a creamy tomato-based soup, I would satisfy all my cravings in one big bowl of steaming love. I made my favorite sandwich into a delicious soup!

Heat a stockpot over medium-high heat until hot. Add the olive oil, onion, and scallions, and sauté for 5 to 8 minutes, just until the onions start to soften. Add the garlic and sauté for 2 minutes.

Lower the heat to medium, add the chopped Roma tomatoes and salt, and simmer for 20 to 25 minutes, until some of the water from the tomatoes has evaporated. Pour in the chicken stock and gently simmer for 40 minutes. Remove the garlic and discard.

In a blender add the cooked tomatoes in batches and blend for 2 minutes each time. Strain the tomatoes in a strainer with small holes (not a mesh strainer). Discard any stray seeds and the pieces of skin that collect in the bottom of the strainer.

Place the pureed tomatoes back into the stockpot, add the milk, and mix well. Adjust the seasoning, adding more salt if necessary, and cook over medium heat for 5 to 8 minutes, until hot.

Ladle the soup into bowls, and divide the bacon, lettuce, heirloom tomato, and toast among the bowls. Add 1 teaspoon of the mayonnaise on top of each. Garnish with the basil and cracked pepper, and serve immediately.

3 tablespoons olive oil

1 medium onion, peeled and sliced thin

2 scallions, chopped

1 clove garlic, peeled and smashed

8 Roma tomatoes, chopped small

1 teaspoon kosher salt

2 cups Roasted Chicken Stock, homemade (page 52), or store-bought organic chicken broth

¾ cup whole milk

10 pieces bacon, fried crisp, crumbled

1 cup head lettuce, chopped small

1 heirloom or round tomato, chopped into 1-inch pieces, seeds discarded

2 slices sourdough bread, toasted, cut into 1-inch cubes

1 tablespoon plus 1 teaspoon mayonnaise mixed with 4 drops Tabasco or hot sauce

5 fresh basil leaves, sliced thin

Cracked pepper

CARAMELIZED CARROT SOUP WITH GREEN APPLES

8 SERVINGS

Soup

3 tablespoons extra-virgin olive oil

1 large yellow onion, peeled and sliced

3 scallions, chopped coarsely

8 medium-size carrots, peeled and chopped into 1-inch pieces

1 teaspoon kosher salt

1 tablespoon fresh minced ginger

2 tablespoons curry powder

2 tablespoons dry sherry

1½ quarts chicken stock, homemade (page 52), or store-bought organic chicken broth

1 (8-ounce) package low-fat cream cheese, cut into pieces

Garnish

1 jalapeño, sliced or diced

2 teaspoons Reduced Balsamic Syrup (page 206)

2 scallions, finely chopped

¼ cup toasted chopped walnuts

½ cup toasted coconut

1 large green apple (see Cook's Note)

Walnut or olive oil for drizzling

2 teaspoons fresh lemon juice for the apple garnish

Don't toss those sad-looking carrots that have been in the fridge a little too long. Whether your carrots are crispy fresh or a little sad, the natural sugar from them and the onions makes this creamy soup slightly sweet, and the curry and garnishes provide kick and robust flavor.

Heat a heavy stockpot on medium-high until hot, 1 minute. Add oil, onion, and scallions, and sauté until the onions start to caramelize, about 8 to 10 minutes. Add carrots, salt, ginger, and curry powder; sauté for 1 minute. Add sherry and chicken stock. Lower the heat so the soup is just boiling. Gently boil until the carrots are tender, about 25 minutes. Test with a small knife: if you can slice through the carrot easily, it's ready.

Puree the soup in a blender in batches: start with a couple of ladlefuls of soup and add half the cream cheese. Cover and puree. Lift the lid and slowly add more soup, a ladleful at a time, until the blender is three-quarters full. Cover and puree for 1 minute, until silky smooth. Pour into a stockpot and repeat the process until all the soup and cream cheese have been pureed.

Add salt and pepper as needed. Garnish with jalapeño, balsamic syrup, scallions, walnuts, coconut, green apple, a drizzle of walnut or olive oil, and a pinch of salt and pepper.

COOK'S NOTES: To toast the walnuts, place them in a cold skillet on medium heat and shake back and forth for about 5 minutes. The nuts are ready when they turn color slightly and release a warm, nutty aroma.

To toast the coconut, preheat the oven to 450°F. Spread ½ cup of shredded coconut on a baking sheet. Bake for 3 to 5 minutes. Check after 2 minutes, shake the pan to loosen the coconut, and flip the flakes over with a metal spatula. Bake 2 minutes more, but keep a close eye on it. Once the coconut starts to toast, it browns quickly.

To prepare the apple garnish, quarter the apple, remove the skin, and core and seed. Chop the apple into small chunks. Place in a bowl, pour 2 teaspoons of lemon juice over, and mix.

TORTILLA SOUP

6 TO 10 SERVINGS

2 quarts chicken stock, homemade (page 52), or store-bought organic chicken broth

½ cup canola oil

8 corn tortillas, cut into strips

1 yellow onion, thinly sliced

1 garlic clove, chopped

½ cup loosely packed cilantro, chopped

1 cup or 1 (6-ounce) can of red plum tomatoes

1 teaspoon cumin

½ teaspoon kosher salt

2 cups bite-size strips roasted chicken breast

2 medium avocados

1 cup shredded sharp cheddar cheese

2 fresh limes, cut into wedges

4 to 5 sprigs fresh cilantro, chopped coarsely

I first tasted tortilla soup years ago in Dallas, Texas, at the Mansion in Turtle Creek, a rather fancy restaurant, beautifully appointed, with a menu to die for. The chef took the very simple idea of using tortillas to give a unique Tex-Mex twist to his soup. Since then, I've ordered tortilla soup every time I've seen it on a menu. I love it, and I serve it often. It's intensely flavorful and completely satisfying.

Make the chicken stock first.

Preheat the oven to 375°F. Lightly coat a sheet pan with canola oil. Place half of the tortilla strips on the sheet pan and bake until golden and crisp, about 5 to 10 minutes. Set aside. Heat a skillet over medium heat. Add ¼ cup of the canola oil. Add the remaining tortilla strips and sauté until they have started to turn golden. Remove the tortillas from the pan and set aside.

Add the remaining oil to the pan. Add onion, and sauté for 2 to 3 minutes. Add garlic and cilantro, and sauté for 30 seconds. In a blender, combine the tomatoes, cumin, and onion mixture. Process until really smooth, about 2 minutes.

Transfer to a large saucepan over medium-low heat. Add the chicken stock and salt, and stir. Cover partially and simmer, stirring occasionally, until the soup is slightly thickened, about 30 to 40 minutes. Add the roasted chicken strips and simmer for 3 to 5 minutes. Taste and adjust the seasoning as needed.

Dice the avocados into bite-size pieces.

To serve, ladle the soup into warmed bowls. Into each portion, sprinkle 2 tablespoons of roasted chicken strips, a handful of cheese, 4 to 5 pieces of avocado, a sprinkle of cilantro, and the tortilla chips. Serve with a lime wedge.

POZOLE

6 TO 8 SERVINGS

For a rich, deep flavor, make this soup with the bones from a roasted chicken. I had my first bowl of pozole a little over a year ago when I went to small café and ordered the soup of the day because it smelled so good. From the first bite, I thought that this was a dish that I just had to have in my repertoire! I never used pork to make soup before, and I was intrigued with the hominy and how it added flavor and texture. I asked for the recipe, but the owner would not give it up, so of course I took it upon myself to come up with a recipe. I think I nailed it.

Make the chicken stock first.

Heat a large stockpot until hot. Add the canola oil, pork, and salt, and sauté until the pork is opaque on all sides, about 5 to 8 minutes. With a slotted spoon, transfer the meat to a bowl and set aside.

Add the onion to the pot, and sauté until it has softened and started to caramelize, 8 to 10 minutes. Add the garlic, chili powder, and cumin, and cook for 1 minute, stirring to blend all the spices evenly. Add the chicken stock, tomatoes, hominy, jalapeño, and sautéed pork. Bring to a boil over high heat. Cover and reduce the heat to low. Simmer slowly for 90 minutes. Taste and adjust the seasoning by adding more salt if necessary.

Just before you are ready to serve, preheat the oven to 400°F. Wrap the tortillas in aluminum foil and bake for 6 to 8 minutes.

Add the diced chicken breast to the simmering soup and heat through until hot. Ladle the soup into bowls and garnish with avocado slices (if you are using), scallions, and cilantro. Serve with a slice of lime and warm tortillas.

3 cups chicken stock, homemade (page 52), or store-bought organic chicken broth

4 tablespoons canola oil

1 pound pork tenderloin, cut into ½-inch pieces

½ teaspoon kosher salt

1 yellow onion, finely chopped

3 garlic cloves, crushed through a garlic press or finely minced

2 tablespoons chili powder

1 teaspoon cumin

1 (28-ounce) can chopped tomatoes

1 (15-ounce) can white hominy, rinsed and drained

1 teaspoon chopped jalapeño

12 corn tortillas

1 cup diced roasted chicken breast

1 avocado, sliced (optional)

2 scallions, chopped

¼ cup cilantro

1 lime, sliced

TUSCAN BREAD SOUP

4 TO 6 SERVINGS

2 cups chicken stock, homemade (page 52), or store-bought organic chicken broth

⅓ cup extra-virgin olive oil

3 garlic cloves, sliced thin

½ teaspoon red pepper flakes

¼ cup dry white wine

2 (28-ounce) cans of crushed tomatoes

1 tablespoon sugar

1½ teaspoons kosher salt

Pepper

2 cups day-old bread such as sourdough baguette, Italian bread, or ciabatta, torn into wide pieces

Garnish

10 fresh basil leaves

¼ teaspoon cracked pepper

Red pepper flakes, for garnish, as much as you can take! (optional)

Freshly grated Romano or Parmesan cheese

Extra-virgin olive oil, for drizzling

Everything you need to make this soup is probably already in your pantry. This is a time and money saver that turns into a great big delicious bowl of convenience. I don't have to turn my stale bread into bread crumbs all the time (unless I need them) because I can also use it to make this hearty soup. I serve it with a salad with a light dressing of extra-virgin olive oil, fresh lemon juice, and a pinch of kosher salt. It's the perfect finishing touch. Oh yes, and a lovely glass of Chianti!

Make the chicken stock first.

Heat a heavy stockpot on medium-high heat. Add the oil, and heat until hot but not smoking. Add garlic and pepper flakes, and sauté until the garlic starts to turn a golden brown (be careful not to burn it).

Add white wine and cook until the wine is almost all evaporated. Add crushed tomatoes, sugar, salt, pepper to taste, and chicken stock. Bring to a gentle boil, reduce heat to low, and simmer uncovered for 30 minutes.

Just before you are ready to serve, add the bread. Mix and heat through, about 5 minutes, to help the bread absorb the soup. Serve in heated bowls. Garnish with basil leaves, cracked pepper, red pepper flakes, and freshly grated cheese. Drizzle olive oil over the top.

HEARTY VEGETABLE MINESTRONE SOUP

6 TO 8 SERVINGS

This minestrone soup is a meal in a bowl—I can get everything I enjoy in one stop. I get the pasta I crave along with beans for protein and good-for-you veggies together in a thick and hearty bowl of soup. A generous portion of Parmesan or Romano cheese is the perfect finishing touch. Talk about feel-good food! It's even better the next day.

Heat a large stockpot over medium-high heat. Add the olive oil and heat until hot. Quickly add the onion, and sauté for 5 minutes, until the onion starts to caramelize. Add the garlic and sauté for 30 seconds.

Add the tomato paste and cook, stirring constantly, for 1 minute; then add the water and stir. Simmer for 2 minutes. Add carrots, celery, zucchini, broccoli florets, cabbage, cauliflower, and salt. Cook for 3 to 5 minutes, until the vegetables start to release their juices.

Add the canned tomatoes and chicken stock. Bring to a gentle boil. Add the beans and stir. Cover and gently simmer on low heat for 45 minutes.

In a blender, in batches, puree three-quarters of the soup until semi-smooth. Pour back into the stockpot and stir well. This will thicken your soup.

Adjust the seasoning (taste for salt; you will probably need to add more—¼ teaspoon at a time, so you don't oversalt). Bring the soup back up to a gentle boil. Add the pasta and stir well so the pasta doesn't stick. Cook the pasta for about 5 minutes or until al dente. You don't want to overcook the pasta. Ladle into heated bowls. Garnish with 2 tablespoons freshly grated cheese per serving, fresh basil, and red pepper flakes to taste. I like to drizzle about a teaspoon of olive oil and balsamic syrup over the top.

⅓ cup olive oil

1 medium onion, diced

2 garlic cloves, minced

2 tablespoons tomato paste

⅓ cup of water

2 carrots, diced

2 celery stalks, diced

2 small zucchini, diced

2 cups broccoli florets, cut small

½ small cabbage, shredded

1 cup cauliflower cut into small pieces

2 teaspoons salt

1 (28-ounce) can of chopped tomatoes

1 quart chicken stock, homemade (page 52), or store-bought organic chicken broth

2 (15-ounce) cans white navy beans or cannellini

1½ cups uncooked small tube, shell-shaped pasta, orzo, or your favorite small pasta

1 cup freshly grated Parmesan or Romano cheese

4 sprigs fresh basil

Red pepper flakes

Extra-virgin olive oil, for drizzling

Reduced Balsamic Syrup (page 206), for drizzling (optional)

PASTA AND RISOTTO

My first solid food as an infant was pasta—pastina, to be exact. Pastina is teeny, tiny bits of pasta shaped like stars. My mother mixed it in my formula and baby cereal, and evidently there was no looking back! As I grew older, Mom would make the pastina with chicken broth, especially when I was under the weather; this soothing soup would automatically made me feel better.

When I was growing up, Wednesdays and Sundays were pasta nights. I use to wonder who made up that rule. I love the smooth, creamy consistency of pasta with eggs, butter, and Parmesan cheese and with different types of tomato sauce, so I felt that *every* day should be pasta day. My mom certainly grew up that way, living in Italy. When my grandmother came to live with us, it all changed; we had pasta at least four or five times a week, and sometimes seven, and I was beyond happy!

There are literally dozens of ways to prepare pasta, with endless sauces using canned or fresh tomatoes, vegetables, salad, fish, grilled meats, cheese, and cream.

I've included several of my grandmother's sauces in this chapter; they've been handed down from generation to generation, and I've tweaked them just a bit to make them my own.

PASTA WITH FRESH ROMA TOMATO SAUCE NO. 1

4 TO 6 SERVINGS

16 (approximately 2¼ pounds) Roma (Italian plum) tomatoes

¼ cup extra-virgin olive oil

8 scallions, chopped

¼ cup white wine

¾ teaspoon kosher salt

2 tablespoons unsalted butter

8 ounces of your favorite semolina pasta

Freshly grated Parmesan cheese

8 medium to large fresh basil leaves, chiffonade (rolled like a cigarette and sliced thin)

A chinoise is a strainer that has the perfect-size holes to strain the tomatoes, just the right size to separate out the skins and seeds.

I make loads of this sauce all year round using Roma tomatoes. I especially love to make it in the summer, when there are so many tomatoes left over from my sister's garden. Of course, if you know how, canning is a great way to always have fresh tomato sauce, even when tomatoes aren't in season.

This quick and easy sauce is creamy and light. It is one of my "bonus" sauces—you can use it as a delicious hot or cold soup.

Cut the tomatoes in quarters, and set aside in a bowl.

Heat a large saucepan on medium-high heat until hot. Add the olive oil and scallions, and cook for 5 minutes. Add the wine and continue to cook, reducing by more than half. Add the tomatoes and salt, and cook for 40 minutes at a slow, bubbly simmer. Remove from heat.

In a food processor, puree the tomato mixture in batches, processing each batch for about 1 minute.

Over a separate saucepan, strain the tomatoes through a chinoise or Chinese cap. Do not use a strainer with tightly woven small mesh; the holes are too small and the resulting puree will be too liquid.

Add butter and taste to see if the sauce needs more salt.

Cook 8 ounces of your favorite semolina pasta according to package directions. (I like penne, farfalle, or linguine with this sauce.) Remember to salt the pasta water.

Drain the pasta well. Pour the drained pasta back into the pot you cooked it in, place the pot back on the stove, and turn the heat to medium-high. Add 1 or 2 ladlefuls of the sauce, and mix to heat through.

Pour the pasta into a serving bowl, and ladle more sauce on top. Sprinkle with plenty of Parmesan cheese and basil.

PASTA WITH FRESH ROMA TOMATO SAUCE NO. 2, MY PERSONAL FAVORITE

4 TO 6 SERVINGS

16 Roma (Italian plum) tomatoes, quartered

2 medium onions, one peeled and quartered and the other peeled and finely chopped, covered, and set aside in the refrigerator

2 small carrots, cut into four pieces

2 celery ribs, cut into four pieces

⅓ cup extra-virgin olive oil

4 scallions, chopped small

4 tablespoons butter

⅓ cup white wine

3 teaspoons kosher salt

8 ounces of your favorite pasta

1 cup freshly grated Parmesan cheese

5 to 6 fresh basil leaves, chopped coarsely

This is my mother's favorite sauce, and I have to say without a doubt mine too. She would tell stories of how when she was little she would pick fresh ripe tomatoes every day, right off the vine in the garden. Her mother would make all kinds of wonderful dishes, but this slightly sweet, delicate sauce was her favorite. My mother is from the northern region of Italy, where the sauces are lighter than the heartier sauces from the south, which is where my dad's family is from.

Whenever I serve this sauce to someone for the first time, the reaction is always the same: one of pure discovery and *Wow!* The aroma is so sweet and fragrant, and the flavor of the sauce so delicate.

In a large sauce pot, combine tomatoes, quartered onion, carrots, and celery, and bring to a boil over medium-high heat. Lower heat to a simmer, cover, leaving the lid slightly open, and simmer for 30 to 45 minutes or until the carrots are soft. Remove from heat.

Puree the vegetables in a blender until smooth.

Over another pot, pass the pureed sauce through a chinois or tomato strainer (page 74) to remove the tomato skins and seeds. Do not use a strainer with tightly woven small mesh; the holes are too small and the resulting puree will be too liquid. Set aside.

Heat a large saucepan on medium heat until warm but not hot. Add the olive oil, finely chopped onions, scallions, and butter. Cook until the onions are translucent (5 to 8 minutes). Add the white wine and continue to cook, reducing by more than half. Add the pureed vegetables and salt, and mix well. Simmer over low heat for 40 minutes.

Cook pasta according to package directions. Drain the pasta and pour into a large warmed pasta serving bowl. Ladle 2 cups of sauce over the pasta, and mix. Ladle 1 more cup over the pasta, or more if you like, and sprinkle on freshly grated Parmesan cheese and fresh chopped basil.

CORKSCREW PASTA WITH SILKY MARINARA SAUCE

4 TO 6 SERVINGS

This is a supereasy and quick sauce with a bit of a bite. It takes 5 minutes to prepare and 25 minutes to cook. Dinner in no time!

Romano cheese goes really well with this sauce. It is a bit saltier than Parmesan (which you can use if you prefer), but it gives this sauce an extra kick to make it rock.

Have all the ingredients lined up and ready to go before you start cooking.

Heat a saucepan on medium-high heat. Add olive oil and garlic, and sauté garlic, turning gently, until it starts to turn golden on all sides. Be careful not to burn the garlic, or the sauce will taste bitter. If this happens, discard and start again. Add the tomatoes, salt, water, sugar, butter, and red pepper flakes. Lower the heat, and simmer for 25 minutes. If the sauce is too thick, add water, ¼ cup at a time. You don't want it watery, but you do want it to have a silky consistency.

Boil the pasta according to the package directions (make sure to salt the water). Cook the pasta until it is al dente, 8 to 10 minutes. Drain well. Return the drained pasta to the pot and place back on the stove.

Remove the garlic from the sauce with a slotted spoon.

Over medium heat, ladle 2 cups of sauce over the pasta and mix well.

Serve the pasta in a heated bowl. Ladle on ¼ cup of sauce, more if you like. Sprinkle on Romano cheese, basil, and additional red pepper flakes if desired.

¼ cup olive oil

2 garlic cloves, peeled and smashed

1 (28-ounce) can chopped canned tomatoes, pureed in a blender for 5 seconds

½ teaspoon kosher salt

⅓ cup water

2 teaspoons sugar

1 tablespoon unsalted butter (optional)

⅛ teaspoon red pepper flakes, plus additional for sprinkling (optional)

8 ounces corkscrew pasta or your favorite pasta

Freshly grated Romano cheese

5 to 6 fresh basil leaves, chopped

COOK'S NOTE: Include ½ cup of frozen baby peas in this sauce if you like. Just add them to the boiling pasta water 10 minutes before the pasta is done.

PAPPARDELLE WITH BOLOGNESE SAUCE

8 TO 10 SERVINGS

This is an authentic, thick, hearty, and meaty sauce that my grandfather use to make. It's great with any pasta, but my favorite is pappardelle. My grandfather would make fresh pappardelle, and I thought it was the best pasta I'd ever had in my whole life. Of course, making your own pappardelle is a bit time-consuming, but you can purchase pappardelle pasta at the market. It's almost as good as Nonno Gino's, but not quite!

Have all your ingredients ready to go.

In a food processor, pulse to chop the onion into small pieces. Set aside. Pulse to chop the carrot and celery into small pieces. Set aside.

Heat a saucepan on medium-high until hot. Add the olive oil and heat for 30 seconds. Add the onions, reduce heat to medium, and sauté for 2 minutes. Add the carrot and celery, and sauté for 2 minutes.

Add the ground chuck and ground pork, breaking up the meat as much as you can. Sprinkle on the salt and pour in the milk, continuing to break up the meat. Cook, reducing the milk until the meat starts to sizzle (about 10 to 15 minutes). Add the wine, and mix well. Continue to cook, reducing the wine by half. Reduce heat to a simmer and add tomato paste. Stir in completely and keep mixing for at least 30 seconds. Add the tomato puree, sugar, and water. Mix well. Cover and simmer on very low heat for 1 hour, stirring often. If you feel the sauce is getting too thick, add more water, ¼ cup at a time.

Cook the pasta according to package directions. Drain well. Pour into a large serving bowl, mix in the sauce, and sprinkle plenty of Parmesan cheese on top. Garnish with basil. Serve immediately.

1 large white onion, quartered

1 small carrot, cut into four pieces

1 celery rib, cut into four pieces

⅓ cup extra-virgin olive oil

1 pound ground chuck

½ pound ground pork

2 teaspoons table salt

1 cup whole milk

⅓ cup white wine

2 tablespoons tomato paste

1 (28-ounce) can tomato puree

1 teaspoon sugar

1½ cups water plus additional as needed

1 pound pappardelle or your favorite pasta

Freshly grated Parmesan cheese

½ cup fresh basil

RIGATONI WITH A HEARTY SIRLOIN SAUCE

6 TO 8 SERVINGS

1 medium white onion, peeled and chopped into quarters

2 scallions, chopped into quarters

1 carrot, chopped into quarters

1 stalk of celery, chopped into quarters

¼ cup plus 2 tablespoons extra-virgin olive oil

1½ pounds sirloin steak, cut into small bite-size pieces

2 teaspoons kosher salt

⅓ cup red wine

1 (6-ounce) can tomato paste

¾ cup water plus additional as needed

1 (28-ounce) can tomato puree

2 tablespoons unsalted butter

2 teaspoons sugar

16 ounces rigatoni or penne pasta

Freshly grated Parmesan cheese

Fresh basil

Red pepper flakes

For this sauce, use 1½ pounds sirloin steak and cut it into small bite-size pieces instead of the ground beef and pork. I like to serve rigatoni or penne pasta with this sauce because I love it when the meat gets stuck in the holes. Sprinkle on plenty of fresh Parmesan cheese!

Have all of your ingredients lined up and ready to go.

In a food processor, combine the onion and scallions, and pulse to chop fine. Repeat the process for the carrot and celery. Place all the vegetables in a bowl, and set aside.

Heat a large sauce pot on medium-high heat. Add ¼ cup of the olive oil, and heat until hot but not smoking. Add the sirloin steak, and sprinkle on the kosher salt. Sear the meat on all sides. Remove the steak and set aside on a plate.

Add the remaining 2 tablespoons of olive oil to the pot and heat until warm. Add the vegetables and sauté for 5 minutes. Add the meat back into the pot, mix well, and sauté for 2 minutes. Pour in the red wine, and reduce until most of the wine has been cooked away.

Lower the heat, add the tomato paste, and stir constantly with a wooden spoon for 1 minute so the paste does not burn. This will help reduce the acid in the tomato paste. After 1 minute, add water and mix thoroughly. Stir in the tomato puree, butter, and sugar. Cover, leaving the lid slightly off center. Simmer on low heat for 50 minutes.

If you find that the sauce is getting too thick, add water ⅓ cup at a time. Taste and adjust seasonings as desired.

Cook the pasta according to directions on the package—al dente is best. Drain well. Pour drained pasta back into the same pot you boiled it in. Return the pot to the stove over medium heat. Ladle two scoops of the sauce over the pasta, and stir for 15 seconds to mix completely, heating through. Pour the pasta into a warmed pasta serving platter. Add the rest of the sauce on top. Sprinkle on freshly grated Parmesan cheese, fresh basil, and red pepper flakes if you like.

FRESH LINGUINE IN A CREAMY LOW-FAT TOMATO SAUCE

6 TO 8 SERVINGS

A note before we start: Imported prosciutto is available in all grocery stores and is not hard to find. Always use the imported prosciutto; it is better in quality and taste than domestic.

There's nothing like homemade fresh pasta, but who has the time to crank it out? I use fresh pasta that I buy at the local market for this recipe. It comes out light and delicate, which provides a nice balance for the sauce's creamy consistency. Most markets carry fresh pasta in the refrigerated section. If you can't find it, you can use boxed linguine; just make sure it's made with semolina flour.

In a food processor, combine onion and scallions, and pulse until finely chopped. Set aside in a bowl. Pulse the carrot, celery, and prosciutto until finely chopped. Add to the onions in the bowl.

Heat a saucepan until hot. Pour in the olive oil and heat through for 30 seconds. Quickly add the chopped vegetables. Sauté until the vegetables start to soften and release their juices, about 5 minutes. Add the wine and reduce until the wine is almost evaporated and you can hear the vegetables start to sizzle. Add the chopped tomatoes, salt, sugar, and water. Mix well. Simmer on low heat, covered, with the lid slightly ajar, for 45 minutes.

Prepare 8 ounces of fresh linguine according to package directions. Five minutes before you are ready to drain the pasta, add the peas to the pasta water and cook with the pasta until the pasta is done.

Drain the pasta and peas and return them to the pot you boiled them in. Over medium heat, pour a couple of ladlefuls of sauce into the pasta and peas. Mix gently with tongs to coat the pasta. Add ½ cup of low-fat milk and ½ cup of Parmesan cheese, and mix. Add the remaining milk and cheese. Mix gently.

Pour into a warm serving bowl (or plate individually), add the remainder of the sauce on top, and spoon on any peas that have fallen to the bottom of the pot. Sprinkle with more cheese and fresh basil.

1 large white onion, quartered

2 scallions, quartered

1 carrot, cut into four pieces

1 celery rib, cut into four pieces

3 slices prosciutto, chopped coarsely

⅓ cup extra-virgin olive oil

⅓ cup dry white wine

1 (28-ounce) can chopped tomatoes in puree

1 teaspoon kosher salt

2 teaspoons sugar

¼ cup water

8 ounces fresh linguine

1 cup freshly cooked or frozen peas

1 cup low-fat milk

1 cup freshly grated Parmesan cheese plus additional for garnish

½ cup chopped fresh basil

Al dente describes pasta and vegetables cooked through but retaining a firm texture and offering a resistance to the bite. I usually cook the pasta a minute less than the directions on the box suggest. All pasta should be cooked this way.

LINGUINE WITH CLAM SAUCE

8 TO 10 SERVINGS

½ cup extra-virgin olive oil

4 garlic cloves, minced

2 cups Italian parsley, loosely packed and finely chopped

¼ teaspoon hot red pepper flakes

2 (6½-ounce) cans minced clams in clam juice

2 tablespoons table salt

1 pound linguine

2 tablespoons fresh lemon juice

8 lemon wedges (optional)

I can't tell you how many times I've reached into my pantry to make this pasta. Not only is it my go-to favorite dish when I need to prepare a meal quickly, but it is an elegant dish to serve for a dinner party. You would never believe the clams are from a can; because they are minced, the clams are not chewy but tender and then seasoned to perfection with extra-virgin olive oil, garlic, and parsley.

Heat a saucepan over medium-high heat for 30 seconds. Add the olive oil, and heat for 1 minute. Add the garlic, parsley, and red pepper flakes, and sauté until the garlic starts to turn golden. (Be careful that you don't burn the garlic or the sauce will taste bitter. If this happens, you need to discard and start again.) Add the minced clams with the juice from the cans. Reduce the heat to medium-low, and simmer for 2 minutes. Turn off the heat, cover, and set aside.

Bring 5 quarts of water with the table salt to a boil in a large pasta pot. Add the linguine and cook the pasta until it is al dente.

Drain the pasta, and give it two good shakes in the colander, but it's not necessary to drain all of the water out. Place the linguine back into the pot you boiled it in, and add the prepared clam sauce and the lemon juice. Turn the heat to medium, and mix using tongs to coat the pasta for 30 seconds. Serve in a heated pasta bowl; garnish with a wedge of lemon.

COOK'S NOTE: To heat the pasta bowl, about 2 minutes before the pasta is ready, pour 4 to 5 ladles of the boiling pasta water into the pasta bowl and let it sit while the pasta continues to cook. Make sure to pour the water out before you add the linguine and clams.

ORECCHIETTE WITH BROCCOLI RABE AND SWEET ITALIAN SAUSAGE

6 SERVINGS

Orecchiette means "little ears" in Italian, and that's what this pasta looks like. I love the shape; it fits perfectly with this dish. Broccoli rabe and sausages make a wonderful flavor combination. The broccoli rabe is a tad bitter and has a bit of a bite. The olive oil and garlic mellow those effects and bring out an outstanding-tasting dish, and the sweet Italian sausages put it over the top.

2 pounds broccoli rabe

4 cups water

⅓ cup extra-virgin olive oil

3 cloves garlic, sliced (not too thin)

1 teaspoon kosher salt

3 sweet Italian sausages

8 ounces orecchiette

½ teaspoon red pepper flakes

3 tablespoons fresh lemon juice

1 lemon, sliced thin

Preheat the oven to 400°F. Cut the stems off the broccoli rabe, along with any discolored leaves.

Bring the water to a boil, add the broccoli rabe, and cover. Boil until tender, about 10 to 15 minutes. Drain in a colander, rinse in cool water, and leave to continue to drain for 5 minutes. Use the back of a wooden spoon to press more water out.

Heat a heavy skillet on high heat. Add the olive oil and the garlic, and sauté just until the garlic starts to turn golden. Immediately add the broccoli rabe, and mix well. Add the salt and mix again. Remove from heat and set aside.

Place the sausages on a baking tray and bake for 30 to 40 minutes, turning at least three times to ensure even cooking. Remove the sausages from the oven and let them rest for 10 minutes before you cut them in 1½-inch pieces.

Cook the pasta according to package directions. Drain the pasta and place it back into the pot you boiled it in. Turn the heat to medium high, add the broccoli rabe, cut-up sausages, and red pepper flakes, and mix well for 1 minute. Add more kosher salt and red pepper flakes if you like, mix in the lemon juice, and garnish with a slice of lemon. Serve immediately.

FARFALLE WITH PESTO

4 TO 6 SERVINGS

1 bunch fresh basil (about 3 cups), rinsed and spun dry

1 bunch Italian parsley (about 2 cups), rinsed and spun dry

2 garlic cloves, peeled

1½ cups extra-virgin olive oil

½ cup toasted pine nuts

8 ounces farfalle (bow-tie pasta)

½ cup freshly grated Parmesan cheese

Parmesan cheese curls (optional)

Red pepper flakes

1 lemon, cut into wedges

I always keep pesto in the fridge. It comes in handy for so many dishes. I love it with pasta and in soups, sauces, egg dishes, and salad dressings.

In the summer, when there is an abundance of basil, I make pesto, pour it into ice cube trays, and freeze it. This way I can always have it on hand.

In a food processor, combine the basil, parsley, and garlic. Process gently. Slowly and gradually add the olive oil until blended.

Place the pine nuts in a small dry frying pan, and cook over medium heat until they start to release their oil, around 5 minutes. Shake the pan back and forth to keep from burning. Set aside.

Cook pasta according to package directions. Drain, reserving ½ cup of the pasta water.

Return the pasta to the pot. Add ½ cup of the pesto and mix well. Add ¼ cup of the reserved pasta water. Add grated Parmesan and toasted pine nuts, and mix well.

Pour into a large serving bowl, and sprinkle on Parmesan curls (if using) and red pepper flakes. Serve immediately or at room temperature, with a lemon wedge on the side.

COOK'S NOTE: You can store pesto in an airtight plastic container or glass jar. It will last for 3 to 4 days in the fridge.

PASTA WITH BROCCOLI

4 TO 6 SERVINGS

Broccoli is my favorite vegetable, and I make it often. I especially love to eat it with pasta—for me, that is heaven: broccoli and pasta together in one bowl, flavored with fruity oil, crisp golden slices of garlic chips, and of course plenty of shaved Parmesan cheese.

Heat a heavy sauce pot until hot. Add ½ cup olive oil and garlic slices. Sauté until golden. Remove from heat and set aside.

Boil the broccoli until tender, and drain well, shaking off excess water.

Place the broccoli in a serving bowl and pour the sautéed garlic and olive oil on top. Mix well, and set aside.

Cook the pasta according to package directions. Drain, reserving 1 cup of pasta water. Do not rinse the pasta. Return the pasta to the pot and place on the stove over medium heat. Add the broccoli, and mix gently until heated through. If you feel you need to add extra water, just add the reserved pasta water ½ cup at a time.

Place the pasta and broccoli in a bowl, and garnish with red pepper flakes, cracked pepper, and Parmesan curls. Sprinkle a pinch of finishing salt, such as fleur de sel, over the top. Drizzle with 2 tablespoons olive oil. Serve with a lemon wedge.

½ cup plus 2 tablespoons extra-virgin olive oil

2 garlic cloves, sliced thin

1 head broccoli, cut into medium-size florets

8 ounces of your favorite pasta

¼ teaspoon red pepper flakes

Cracked pepper

Shaved Parmesan cheese, enough to sprinkle over 6 servings

Fleur de sel

1 lemon, cut into wedges

COOK'S NOTE: To make Parmesan cheese curls, use a cheese slicer or vegetable peeler.

QUICK VERSION OF PASTA WITH PROSCIUTTO AND PEAS

4 TO 6 SERVINGS

2 cups frozen baby peas

1 large onion, sliced thin

2 cups canned chopped tomatoes

2 slices prosciutto, finely chopped

1 tablespoon extra-virgin olive oil

1 teaspoon kosher salt

8 ounces rigatoni or penne

2 tablespoons unsalted butter

1 cup freshly grated Parmesan cheese plus additional for sprinkling

Cracked pepper

This is what I call one of my "dump recipes" because that's what you do. It takes 10 minutes to prepare; you just dump all the ingredients into a pot. Forty-five minutes later, you have a delicious sauce. Best of all, the ingredients are staple items (page 219) that I always have on hand.

In a sauce pot, combine the peas, onion, tomatoes, prosciutto, olive oil, and salt. Cover, and simmer over medium heat, just under a boil, for 30 to 45 minutes.

Cook the pasta according to package directions. Drain the pasta and return it to the pot you boiled it in. Over medium heat, add all the sauce to the pot with the pasta. Mix gently so you won't squash the peas. Heat through for about 30 seconds. Add the butter and the Parmesan cheese, and mix gently but well. Remove from heat.

To serve, pour into a serving bowl, sprinkle with Parmesan cheese, and crack a nice portion of pepper over the top.

RISOTTO

6 TO 8 SERVINGS

This is a delicious stand-alone dish, and I often serve it in place of pasta to start off the meal. My favorite way to present this smooth, creamy, slightly nutty-tasting risotto, however, is with my fork-tender Osso Buco (page 132). The combination is a winner, and my friends often ask me when they know they are coming to our home for dinner if I would make osso buco over risotto! My pleasure!

Combine the chicken broth and saffron in a saucepan and bring to a boil. Cover and keep warm over low heat.

Heat a stock pot over medium-high heat until warm (about 30 seconds). Add oil, butter, onions, and salt. Sauté just until the onions turn translucent and are soft, about 8 to 10 minutes. Add the rice and cook, stirring frequently, for 4 minutes.

Add 2 cups of the warm broth and the white wine to cover the rice. Mix well. Bring to a gentle boil over low heat, and boil gently until the liquid is almost gone.

Stir in 3 more cups of broth, stirring about every 3 minutes, and simmer until the liquid is absorbed.

Add 1½ cups more broth, ½ cup every 3 to 4 minutes, to keep the rice mixture creamy.

Continue to cook, stirring frequently, until the rice is cooked through but still a bit firm in the center, about 10 to 12 minutes. Stir in the Parmesan cheese and lemon zest, and adjust the seasoning. Serve immediately.

6½ cups chicken stock, homemade (page 52), or store-bought organic chicken broth, heated through

½ teaspoon saffron

3 tablespoons extra-virgin olive oil

6 tablespoons unsalted butter

1 medium yellow onion, diced small

½ teaspoon kosher salt

2 cups arborio rice

1 cup dry white wine

1 cup grated Parmesan cheese

Zest from 1 lemon

COOK'S NOTE: Risotto is one of my favorites. The thing I love about a beautiful bowl of creamy risotto is that you can add different fresh vegetables.

I love the combination of fresh asparagus tips, sliced baby zucchini, and fresh garden peas. I add them raw 5 minutes before the risotto is finished.

Making a risotto with porcini mushrooms will score major points. Grilled seafood such as shrimp along with saffron is a winning combination too! Try adding your favorite vegetable to your risotto.

MACARONI AND CHEESE WITH TRUFFLE OIL— OR NOT

6 TO 8 SERVINGS

4 tablespoons unsalted butter

4 tablespoons all-purpose flour

3½ cups warm milk

½ teaspoon kosher salt

Cracked pepper

3 cups shredded extra-sharp cheddar cheese

4 ounces goat cheese, cut up

2 tablespoons truffle oil (optional)

8 ounces of your favorite macaroni

½ cup grated Parmesan cheese

"Macaroni and cheese." That's it; that's all you have to say to get everyone running to the table, saying, "Ooooh, my favorite—I love it!"

You can put a different spin on the traditional by adding truffle oil. The oil gives the dish a woodsy flavor with a heady aroma. This particular recipe has gotten a thumbs-up response from my family and friends.

If the truffle oil is too overwhelming for your taste, just leave it out— but I really think you'll be missing a treat!

In a small saucepan, melt the butter. Stir in the flour, and mix to form a roux. Add half of the warm milk, and mix well, using a whisk to make sure you get the ingredients off the sides and bottom of the saucepan. Add the rest of the milk. Using a wooden spoon, continuously stir the sauce until it begins to thicken and tiny bubbles form on the sides (5 to 6 minutes). Do not boil. Add salt and pepper to taste. Add cheddar cheese and goat cheese. Mix until the cheese is completely melted and the sauce is smooth. Add the truffle oil, and mix well. Cover and set aside.

Cook the macaroni according to package directions.

Preheat the broiler. Spray a 4-quart casserole dish or pie plate with cooking spray.

Place the cooked and drained macaroni in a large bowl, and pour the cheese mixture over it, mixing well. Spoon the mixture into the casserole. Sprinkle Parmesan cheese over the top, and broil until the top is crusty and golden, about 6 to 10 minutes. Watch carefully, to be sure it doesn't burn.

Serve immediately.

CHICKEN

There are so many wonderful ways to prepare chicken. I love that I can make three meals from one 5-pound chicken! I use the bones from a roasted chicken to make stock that I always keep on hand for hearty soups, sauces, pasta, risotto, and roasts. The meat from the chicken will provide many wonderful dishes. I've provided many suggestions in this chapter on how to "stretch" your chicken and what to do with leftovers. You'll be surprised at how many dishes you can come up with!

I buy only organic chicken, and I serve it at least three times a week because it is so versatile. I have it for lunch, grilled, along with a fresh garden salad or a toasted warm panini sandwich and a big, beautiful bowl of piping hot chicken soup. I never tire of eating chicken because there are so many unique and delicious ways to prepare it. I included only nine recipes in this chapter . . . but I could easily add nine more!

CHICKEN PICCATA

6 SERVINGS

This is one of the easiest and quickest of recipes. I serve this dish often at dinner parties because it cooks in no time and it's delicately flavored with white wine, lemon, and capers.

I serve it over Creamy Yukon Gold Mash with Scallions (page 158), rice, or couscous.

Sprinkle both sides of the chicken breasts with kosher salt and pepper to taste. Dredge the chicken in the flour.

Heat the oil in a large frying pan over medium-high heat. Add the garlic, and sauté until golden in color. (Be careful not to burn the garlic or it will taste bitter.) Remove the garlic from the oil and discard. Quickly add the chicken and sauté 3 minutes on each side. Add the white wine, scraping the bottom and sides of the pan to incorporate any of the small bits that have collected. Cook until the wine is almost gone. Add the lemon juice over the chicken. Lower heat to a simmer and cover, leaving the lid slightly ajar to let the steam escape. Simmer 2 minutes more on each side.

Remove from pan, and season with a pinch more kosher salt and pepper. Place the sliced lemons on top of the cutlets, and sprinkle with capers and fresh parsley. Serve over mashed potatoes.

3 organic chicken breasts, skinned, boned, and pounded to ¼-inch thickness (your butcher will do this for you if you ask)

Kosher salt

Cracked pepper

1 cup all-purpose flour, for dredging

¼ cups extra-virgin olive oil

3 garlic cloves, crushed

½ cup white wine

Juice of 1 lemon

1 lemon, sliced thin

¼ cup capers

¼ cup chopped Italian parsley

COOK'S NOTE: You probably will have to use two frying pans to prepare this dish because you won't be able to put all 6 pieces of chicken at once into one pan. It's important not to crowd the chicken while you sauté because the chicken will steam and become gummy. If you don't have two frying pans, make the chicken in batches. When you finish the first batch, cover it lightly with aluminum foil and wipe out the bottom of the pan with a paper towel before you go on to the second.

CHICKEN BREASTS FRIED GOLDEN, JUICY, AND CRUNCHY!

6 SERVINGS

3 organic chicken breasts

5 cups buttermilk

2 tablespoons Tabasco

1 teaspoon cayenne pepper

3 cups panko (Japanese-style bread crumbs)

1½ teaspoons garlic salt

1½ teaspoons onion salt

1½ teaspoons kosher salt

1 teaspoon pepper

1½ cups rice flour

2 eggs, beaten

3 cups canola or vegetable oil

Lemon slices, for garnish

I accidently let the chicken marinate for two days, and I thought I would have to toss it, but the buttermilk acted as a tenderizer. I fried up a batch, and I have never, ever had fried chicken so tender and moist. If you don't want to wait two days, try to marinate at least overnight!

Who doesn't like fried chicken? This recipe makes crunchy, moist, and light fried chicken.

Slice the chicken breasts in half, cut off the tenderloins from the back of the breasts, and place the breasts, including the tenderloins, in a bowl.

To make the marinade, combine the buttermilk, Tabasco, and cayenne pepper. Mix well, then pour over the chicken to coat. Pour the chicken and marinade into a large plastic bag and seal. (I use two plastic bags in case of leaks.) Lay the bag flat in the refrigerator for 24 hours (no longer than two days). Make sure to turn it at least once to redistribute the buttermilk. The buttermilk breaks down the protein in the chicken, rendering it tender and moist.

Prepare the panko bread crumb mixture. In a large plastic bag, combine the panko, garlic salt, onion salt, kosher salt, and pepper. Close the bag and shake well.

Remove chicken from marinade and let the excess marinade drip off; then place chicken in a bowl. Discard marinade.

Coat the chicken in the rice flour, dip it in the beaten eggs, and coat it with the panko mixture. Place on a cooling rack and let air dry for about 30 minutes. (You can fry immediately if you wish, but letting the chicken air dry helps with the crunchiness—your call.)

When ready to fry, heat the canola oil in a cast-iron or heavy skillet over medium-high heat until hot but not smoking. To test to see if the oil is ready, take a pinch of coating off the chicken and drop it in the oil. If it starts to bubble briskly, it's ready for the chicken. Carefully place the chicken in the hot oil, reduce the heat to medium-low, and fry for 2 to 3 minutes per side, up to 8 minutes, or until the panko coating has turned a beautiful golden color. If the panko starts to brown too fast, reduce the heat to low.

Drain on a paper towel. Place the chicken on a rack and let sit for 5 minutes before serving, so it will retain its juices. Garnish with a few slices of lemon, and enjoy!

CHICKEN ROASTED TO PERFECTION

6 TO 8 SERVINGS

I serve this chicken often, and it always gets major compliments.

While the chicken is roasting, it sends a mouthwatering aroma through the entire house. When it comes out of the oven, it's golden and crispy on the outside, moist and tender on the inside.

The secret is the marinade, which turns into a superdelicious pan sauce you can pour all over the chicken—and over the mashed potatoes, if you are serving them.

The other secret is to baste often. I know the cooking time may seem long, and it is—3 hours for a 6-pound chicken—but if you baste it as often as I suggest, every half hour or so, you will have a tender, fall-off-the-bone, mouthwatering chicken!

I like to marinate the chicken in a large ziplock bag overnight in the refrigerator, but if you don't have time to do that, you can pour the marinade over the chicken and bake right away.

Make the chicken stock first.

Remove gizzards, heart, neck, and liver from the cavity of the chicken. Rinse the chicken well inside and out. Pat dry and place in a large ziplock bag.

To make the marinade, whisk together Dijon mustard, olive oil, lemon juice, and soy sauce. Add the garlic and mix well.

Stuff the lemon rind into the chicken cavity along with half of the fresh parsley, rosemary, and thyme, if using. Preheat the oven to 350°F.

Place the chicken in a heavy roasting pan. Wrap the tips of the drumsticks and the wings in small pieces of foil to protect them from burning while roasting. Pour the marinade over the bird and top with the remaining fresh herbs, if using, or sprinkle the dry herbs on the chicken. Cover (you can use heavy-duty aluminum foil if you don't have a lid for the roasting pan). Seal tightly. Try to make sure the aluminum foil is not resting on top of the skin, or it will stick and come off when you remove the foil; leave an air pocket. Roast for 90 minutes with the foil on. Then remove the foil and continue to roast for an additional 30 minutes.

3 cups chicken stock, homemade (page 52), or store-bought organic chicken broth

6-pound whole organic chicken, rinsed and dried

¾ cup Dijon mustard

3 tablespoons olive oil

Juice from 1 fresh lemon; keep lemon rind for stuffing

⅓ cup light soy sauce

2 garlic cloves, crushed

Several sprigs fresh parsley, or 1 tablespoon dry parsley

Several sprigs fresh rosemary, or 1 tablespoon dry rosemary

Several sprigs fresh thyme, or 1 tablespoon dry thyme

¼ cup chopped fresh Italian parsley

You can usually buy fresh herbs already bundled as poultry seasoning. If they're not available, dry herbs are fine.

So here's the deal with chicken: I cook and eat a lot of it—so much so that I'm naturally concerned about the way the chickens are raised and nourished. That's why I buy only organic cage-free chickens. Yes, they're more expensive, but I think it's worth it—for me and my family, and for the chickens.

Add 2 cups chicken stock. Using a wooden spoon, scrape the bottom of the roasting pan to loosen the bits that have collected on the sides and bottom of the pan. Baste the chicken well. Continue roasting uncovered for 60 minutes, basting every 15 minutes. Add chicken stock, if needed, a ladleful at a time to keep the bottom of the pan from burning.

Remove the chicken from the oven. Remove the chicken from the roasting pan and place it on a carving board to rest for 10 minutes before carving. Cover lightly with foil.

Add ½ cup chicken stock to the roasting pan, and stir to release any crusty bits that have collected on the bottom and sides of the pan. Place a strainer over another pot, and pour the juices from the roasting pan through the strainer. Remove the strainer and discard its contents. Skim off any oil that has risen to the top of the pan juices.

Carve the chicken, pour the pan juices over the meat, and sprinkle with chopped parsley.

CORNISH GAME HENS

8 SERVINGS

I love to serve this elegant dish for special occasions; it makes a beautiful, impressive presentation and is so delicious.

You can serve it over Creamy Yukon Gold Mash with Scallions (page 158) with sautéed spinach on the side. A butter leaf salad (Butter Lettuce with Feta, Walnuts, and Olive Oil and Lemon Dressing, page 46) is the perfect starter.

Rinse the hens and pat dry. Using kitchen shears, cut the hens in half up the middle. Place in a glass or ceramic bowl to marinate.

Whisk together in a glass bowl the olive oil, mustard, soy sauce, teriyaki sauce, lemon juice, and garlic. Pour the marinade over the hens. Cover tightly with aluminum foil and leave in the refrigerator for at least two hours. (You can even leave them overnight.)

Preheat the oven to 350°F. Place the hens in a roasting pan, cut side down. Pour the marinade on top. Cover tightly with foil, and roast for 45 minutes. Remove foil and baste every fifteen minutes for 1 hour. If you notice that the roasting pan is dry, add chicken stock, one ladleful at a time, to make sure there is enough liquid in the bottom of the roasting pan. By the time you remove the hens from the oven, they should have a rich, dark caramel color and the meat should come off the bone easily.

To serve, remove the hens from the oven and place them on a warm platter. Cover with foil to keep warm while you prepare the gravy.

Add 1 tablespoon of the arrowroot to 2 tablespoons cold water, mix, and pour into the roasting pan. Add 2 cups chicken stock and the sherry. Stir, scraping all the bits from the sides of the pan. Strain through a wire mesh strainer, and pour into a saucepan.

Again, mix 1 tablespoon arrowroot with 2 tablespoons cold water. Pour into the saucepan. Bring the gravy to a gentle boil until it starts to thicken slightly. Add salt and pepper to taste. Pour the gravy over the hens, and garnish with parsley and lemon zest.

4 Cornish game hens

2 tablespoons extra-virgin olive oil

1 tablespoon Dijon mustard

½ cup low-sodium soy sauce

½ cup teriyaki sauce

Juice from 2 fresh lemons

2 cloves garlic, smashed

3 cups chicken broth

2 tablespoons arrowroot

1 tablespoon dry sherry or white wine

Kosher salt

Cracked pepper

½ cup loosely packed chopped Italian parsley

Zest of 1 lemon

FALL-OFF-THE-BONE ROASTED CHICKEN THIGHS

6 SERVINGS

I'm a dark-meat lover, and I love chicken thighs. These are roasted until the meat falls off the bone.

I usually double this recipe because I like to have plenty of leftover thigh meat; it makes great sandwiches, tacos, and taco salads and is delicious shredded in soup.

A vegetable couscous is lovely with this dish.

Make the chicken stock first.

Preheat the oven to 350°F.

Place chicken thighs in a baking dish.

Combine Dijon mustard, lemon juice, soy sauce, and olive oil, and pour over the chicken. Turn the thighs to coat evenly.

Sprinkle on the fines herbes and the fennel seeds; then sprinkle on several pinches of kosher salt and plenty of cracked pepper.

Cover with aluminum foil, and roast for 45 minutes. Remove the foil and baste. Add 2 cups of chicken stock and stir to turn up any of the bits that have formed at the bottom of the roasting pan. Baste again with a bulb baster.

Continue to roast for 60 minutes more, basting every 15 minutes to keep the chicken supermoist. The thighs will turn a beautiful caramel color. If you find that the bottom of the roasting pan is dry, add the rest of the chicken stock.

3 cups chicken stock, homemade (page 52), or store-bought organic chicken broth

12 chicken thighs, washed and dried

⅓ cup Dijon mustard

¼ cup fresh lemon juice

⅓ cup low-sodium soy sauce

2 tablespoons olive oil

2 tablespoons fines herbes

1 teaspoon fennel seeds

Kosher salt

Cracked pepper

COOK'S NOTE: I always try to use fresh herbs such as oregano, rosemary, thyme, parsley, and sage in all my cooking, but I like using dried fines herbes for this. You can find them in the spice aisle of your market. I like that fact that the herbs are tiny and can be baked right on the skin, giving the chicken and the pan juices a more intense flavor.

CHICKEN CROQUETTES WITH FETA CHEESE FILLING

12 SERVINGS

3 eggs

¼ cup Parmesan cheese

¼ cup Romano cheese

2 cups diced roasted chicken

1 tablespoon chopped Italian parsley

½ cup mashed potatoes, homemade or store-bought

½ teaspoon kosher salt

1 cup feta cheese; you can use goat cheese instead if you like

1 cup Wondra flour

2 cups plain bread crumbs

2 cups canola oil

2 lemons, cut into wedges

Fresh thyme, for garnish (optional)

My mom and grandmother would make croquettes out of almost any leftover beef, lamb, or fish, but my favorite croquettes are made with chicken. I like to eat them right out of the frying pan, while they're still sizzling hot, with a squeeze of fresh lemon juice and a sprinkle of kosher salt. The crunchy layers outside along with the fluffy hot insides with oozing cheese make my head swim!

I use these croquettes in my Nontraditional Greek Salad (page 45).

Combine 1 egg with the Parmesan and Romano cheese, and beat well.

In a food processor, combine roasted chicken, egg with cheese mixture, parsley, mashed potatoes, and salt. Process until uniform and smooth.

Using about ¼ cup of the chicken mixture, create a cylinder that will fit into the palm of your hand. Pull the cylinder open to form two halves, and with your thumb press a hole in each half. Place a piece of feta or goat cheese the size of a large grape in one half and cover it up with the other half. Shape back into a cylinder, making sure the cheese is surrounded by the chicken so it doesn't ooze out during frying. Continue to make croquettes with the remainder of the chicken mixture (about a dozen croquettes).

Place the croquettes on a platter, cover with plastic wrap, and refrigerate for 1 hour. (The croquettes can be kept covered in the refrigerator for up to 2 days before frying.)

When you're ready to cook the croquettes, beat the remaining two eggs. Line up the Wondra flour, the beaten eggs, and the bread crumbs. Roll a croquette first in the flour, then in the beaten eggs, and finally in the bread crumbs, making sure you have covered the whole croquette with the crumbs. Place on a baking rack while you coat the rest of the croquettes. When all of the croquettes are ready to fry, place canola oil in a frying pan over medium-high heat until hot (about 5 to 6 minutes). You can check to see if the oil is hot enough to start frying by breaking a tiny piece of croquette off and dropping it in the oil. If it starts to bubble

and sizzle, the oil is hot enough. Lower heat to medium, and fry the croquettes until they are golden brown on all sides. Keep an eye out so they don't burn; you want the crust to be a deep golden brown. Drain croquettes on a paper towel.

Croquettes can be served right out of the frying pan, while they are still sizzling hot, with lemon wedges on the side, fresh thyme, and a pinch of kosher salt. They can also be served at room temperature and are delicious cold, right out of the refrigerator.

CHICKEN MARSALA WITH ANGEL HAIR PASTA

8 TO 10 SERVINGS

1 cup all-purpose flour

3 (4- to 5-ounce) whole organic chicken breasts, boned and pounded into ¼-inch thickness (ask your butcher to do this for you)

½ teaspoon kosher salt

Cracked pepper

7 tablespoons olive oil

2 medium yellow onions, sliced thin

2 whole red peppers, seeded and sliced thin

½ ounce whole mushrooms; I prefer cremini—they look like small button mushrooms but they are deep brown

4 whole garlic cloves, smashed

⅓ cup marsala wine

Juice from 2 fresh lemons

1 cup Roasted Chicken Stock, homemade (page 52), or store-bought organic chicken broth

8 ounces angel hair pasta

¼ cup chopped fresh Italian parsley

2 scallions, chopped

Reduced Balsamic Syrup (page 206)

This is one of my favorites of the dishes my grandmother use to make when we had company, which seemed like all the time! The only thing I've changed is that I serve it with angel hair instead of linguine because the angel hair is much lighter. The sauce is thick, with a touch of sweetness from the marsala, so the angel hair is a perfect complement.

Have all of your ingredients ready to go.

Place the flour in a shallow dish, and set aside.

Sprinkle both sides of the chicken breasts with kosher salt and pepper. Set aside.

Heat a heavy skillet until hot. Add 2 tablespoons of the olive oil and swirl it around the pan. Add the onions and peppers and sauté until the onions are translucent, about 4 to 5 minutes. Add the mushrooms and sauté the vegetables until they have started to caramelize, about 6 to 7 minutes. Sprinkle on ¼ teaspoon kosher salt, and mix well. Pour the vegetables into a bowl, and set aside.

Clean the frying pan; you're going to use it again. Dredge the chicken in flour and set aside. Place the pan back on the stove over medium-high heat. Add 3 tablespoons of oil, and swirl it around the pan. Add the garlic, and sauté until golden. Remove the garlic from the skillet and discard. Add the floured chicken breasts, and sauté until a golden crust forms on the bottom of the chicken (about 3 minutes). Turn the chicken and sauté the other side for 3 minutes. Add the marsala, and cook until the wine is almost gone. Add 3 tablespoons lemon juice, sautéed vegetables, and chicken stock. Cover, lower heat, and simmer for 30 minutes.

When ready to serve, cook the angel hair according to package directions. Drain the pasta, reserving 1 cup of pasta water. Pour the pasta into a serving bowl, and add the remainder of the olive oil (2 tablespoons), 1 cup of pasta water, the remaining lemon juice, and parsley, and mix. Serve the chicken marsala either over the angel hair or on the side. Garnish with parsley and the scallions. Drizzle on balsamic syrup.

"BEST EVER" CHICKEN CHILI

6 SERVINGS

This thick and hearty bowl of chili is lean and mean and low in fat. It tastes even better the next day.

In a small bowl, combine chili powder, cayenne, and cumin.

Heat a heavy-bottomed sauce pot until hot. Add the canola oil and heat until hot. Add the onions and scallions, sauté for 5 minutes, then add the garlic and sauté for 30 seconds. Add the ground chicken and salt. Add the chili powder mixture, and mix.

Using a metal spatula, break up the chicken into small pieces.

Add milk, and reduce until the chicken starts to sizzle. Lower heat to a simmer, add tomato paste, and stir completely. Keep mixing for at least 30 seconds. Add the chopped tomatoes, corn, and kidney beans, and mix well.

Serve in a deep-dish bowl, garnished with a dollop of low-fat sour cream, cilantro, crushed tortilla chips, and chopped jalapeño.

Chili

2 tablespoons ancho chili powder

⅛ teaspoon cayenne pepper

1 tablespoon cumin

4 tablespoons canola oil

2 medium onions, chopped

4 scallions, chopped

2 garlic cloves, minced

1½ pounds ground dark-meat chicken

2 teaspoons kosher salt

1 cup low-fat milk

2 tablespoons tomato paste

1 (28-ounce) can chopped tomatoes

1 ear fresh corn kernels, scrapped of the cob, or 1 cup canned or frozen corn

1 (15-ounce) can kidney beans

Garnish

6 tablespoons sour cream

½ cup loosely packed cilantro, coarsely chopped

Handful tortilla chips, to crush over the chili

1 to 2 jalapeños, seeded and chopped

COOK'S NOTE: You can use this chili as a sauce for pasta or even in a lasagna. Really, all you need is the low-fat ricotta, fresh Parmesan cheese, and lasagna noodles; put it together and bake!

CHICKEN POTPIE WITH CORN-BREAD CRUST

4 TO 6 SERVINGS

For me, chicken potpie is predictable and boring! The crust, traditionally a piecrust, doesn't do it for me. I like saving my piecrusts for pies filled with juicy, fruity goodness.

This corn-bread crust is a wonderful alternative and seems to go with the creaminess of the filling. I like it better!

Boil the potatoes and carrots until tender but not soft, and set aside.

Spray a 2-quart casserole with cooking spray or coat lightly with butter.

For the filling, heat a large saucepan until hot, add the oil, butter, and onions. Sauté onions until they are soft, about 5 minutes. Sprinkle in the flour and mix. Slowly pour in the chicken stock, whisking well with a wire whisk. Still using the whisk, cook the mixture over medium heat until thickened and bubbly, about 2 to 3 minutes. Add the chopped chicken, peas, cooked potatoes and carrots, salt, pepper to taste, and Tabasco. Cook on medium heat until the mixture is heated through, about 2 to 3 minutes. Turn into the prepared casserole dish, spreading evenly.

Preheat the oven to 400°F.

For the crust, in a bowl combine cornmeal, flour, baking powder, sugar, and salt. In a small bowl combine the milk, oil, and egg yolk. Add to the dry ingredients, and mix until uniform but a bit lumpy. Spoon the batter evenly over the filling.

Bake until the top is golden brown, about 22 to 25 minutes.

Filling

2 cups chopped potatoes

½ cup chopped carrots

1 tablespoon olive oil

1 tablespoon unsalted butter

1 medium onion, chopped

¼ cup all-purpose flour

2 cups chicken stock, homemade (page 52), or store-bought organic chicken broth

2 cups chopped roasted chicken breast

½ cup frozen baby peas

1 teaspoon kosher salt

Cracked pepper

Dash of Tabasco sauce

Corn-bread crust

¾ cup cornmeal

¾ cup all-purpose flour

1 tablespoon baking powder

1½ tablespoons sugar

½ teaspoon salt

¾ cup low-fat milk

2 tablespoons canola oil

1 large egg yolk, slightly beaten

COOK'S NOTE: I also like to make this recipe using individual ramekins. Place 12 ramekins on a baking sheet. Spray butter-flavored cooking spray all over the insides, and fill the ramekins three-quarters of the way up with the chicken mixture. Top with 2 tablespoons of the corn-bread batter and spread to cover the filling. Bake at 400°F for 10 to 12 minutes or until the corn bread is puffed up and golden.

BEEF AND LAMB

My dad made his living as a butcher and would always bring home the best cuts of meat that weren't too expensive. Every so often he would bring home T-bone steaks (his favorite); he would personally grill them on the backyard grill, and they always turned out perfect. My mom would make incredible dishes that drove me crazy while they were cooking. Whether the aroma came from meatballs simmering in a sauce, a meat loaf baking, a roast caramelizing in the oven, or a skirt steak sizzling in the frying pan, it never failed to make my mouth water and get me excited about dinner. My mom and grandmother were genius at preparing beef, then using the leftovers—if there were any—to make other great-tasting beef dishes.

This chapter is devoted to fabulous and economical ways to use ground beef and lamb and inexpensive cuts of meat that are tender and rich in flavor. I'll also show you how to use expensive cuts of meat and still be able to feed your whole family without having to cut into your budget.

KICK-BUTT CHILI

8 TO 10 SERVINGS

Chili

3 tablespoons canola oil

2 pounds chuck roast, minced for chili

3 onions, finely chopped

4 garlic cloves, minced

5 tablespoons chili powder

1 jalapeño, seeded and finely chopped

2 teaspoons ground coriander

2 tablespoons ground cumin

2 cups organic beef stock (boxed or canned)

1 cup dark beer

1 (28-ounce) can chopped tomatoes

½ cup fresh roasted corn or canned corn

1 (15-ounce) can of black beans, rinsed and drained

1 (15-ounce) can of pinto beans, rinsed and drained

1 tablespoon masa

Kosher salt

Cracked pepper

Garnish

1¼ cups sour cream

½ cup chopped scallions

¼ cup chopped cilantro

2 cups grated cheddar cheese

2½ teaspoons hot red chili flakes

1 cup crushed tortilla chips (optional)

2 jalapeños, seeded and chopped or sliced (optional)

This chili is hearty without feeling heavy, and all the flavors blend so well together! It's a huge hit on Super Bowl Sunday, but I serve it all year round for lunch or dinner with a simple salad.

For the greatest results, purchase a chuck roast and tell your butcher you want the beef minced for chili.

Heat a cast-iron frying pan or heavy-bottomed skillet over medium heat. Add 1 tablespoon of canola oil and half of the meat, and brown for about 8 minutes. Pour the meat into a strainer positioned over a bowl, and let the fat drain. Set the strained meat aside. Wipe down the frying pan using a paper towel, cleaning off the residual oil and bits of beef from the bottom. Heat 1 tablespoon of canola oil in the frying pan and cook and drain the remaining beef using the same process. Discard the drained fat.

In a large sauce pot, heat 1 tablespoon of oil until hot. Add the onions and sauté just until translucent, about 5 to 8 minutes. Add the garlic and sauté until it just begins to turn golden. Add the chili powder, jalapeño, coriander, and cumin, and mix well. Cook for 30 seconds. Add the beef stock, beer, tomatoes, corn, black and pinto beans, and cooked beef. Cover and simmer on low heat for 1 hour, giving it a stir every 15 minutes. Add the masa to thicken the chili to the perfect consistency, and simmer for 10 minutes. Season with kosher salt and pepper to taste.

Serve in heated bowls, and garnish each serving with 2 tablespoons sour cream, 1 to 2 teaspoons scallions, 1 teaspoon cilantro, 2 to 3 tablespoons cheddar cheese, ⅛ to ¼ teaspoon hot red chili flakes, and crushed tortilla chips (if using) or a thick slice of your favorite corn bread. The jalapeños are optional, but go ahead and do it! Wash everything down with an ice-cold beer.

SLIDERS

2 DOZEN SLIDERS

2 packages (about 12 per package) Hawaiian dinner rolls or whole wheat hamburger buns

2 pounds chuck roast (have your butcher grind it fresh)

Kosher salt

Cracked pepper

6 slices sharp cheddar cheese, cut into quarters, at room temperature

Ketchup, squeezed right from the bottle

Bread-and-butter pickles

These miniburgers are insanely good. Whenever I make them, I can't keep up with the demand—they're a major hit! They're my newest addition to Super Bowl Sunday, and I swear these burgers get as much attention as the game. They're also a great last-minute meal that will satisfy your whole family. You will be surprised how far a little bit of beef goes. Before I bring the burgers out I serve a cup of hearty soup and then serve these tasty, juicy morsels with coleslaw and potato salad.

With a 2-inch biscuit cutter, cut slider-size buns out of the dinner rolls. If the buns are too thick (they will be if you are using Hawaiian dinner rolls), just press down to flatten them before using the biscuit cutter. They will bounce back just a little, leaving you with the perfect buns.

Shape the sliders by rolling golf ball–size meatballs between your palms, then pressing them into 2-inch-wide patties ¾ inch thick. You should have enough beef to make 16 to 18 miniburgers, maybe more. Sprinkle both sides of the sliders with kosher salt and pepper.

Heat a grill pan or heavy skillet until searing hot. Brush a tablespoon of canola oil over the grill pan. Sprinkle the miniburgers with kosher salt. Place the miniburgers salt side down on the grill, and sprinkle the tops of the burgers with kosher salt. Grill for 1½ minutes on each side, then flip over once more and add a slice of cheese on top of each burger. Grill for 1 minute, until the cheese has melted (if you have a large enough lid, cover the burgers, as this will help the cheese melt quicker). Transfer the burgers to a warm platter.

Grill the buns on the same grill pan, lightly toasting the inside tops and bottoms only (about 15 to 20 seconds).

To assemble the burger, put a squirt of ketchup and a pickle on the bottom bun, add the burger, and cover with the top bun. Serve immediately and wait for the compliments!

STRETCHING
THE MAIN INGREDIENT

The next few recipes show you how to do what I love to do best, and that is make extraordinary, easy, and flavorful meals by stretching the main ingredient. The main ingredient here, of course, is beef—ground beef to be exact. From a 5- to 6-pound chuck roast I show you how to make 6 (4-ounce) melt-in-your-mouth cheeseburgers, 12 meatballs in a delicious tomato sauce, and a juicy meat loaf. This is a great way to save money and time.

I suggest you prepare and enjoy the cheeseburgers (page 116) the same day you purchase the beef only because the flavor of the beef after it has been freshly ground is robust and full. The secret to tender, moist, juicy cheeseburgers, meatballs, and meat loaf is to pick a 5- to 6-pound chuck roast and ask your butcher to grind it for hamburger. You will totally taste the difference in texture and freshness; you are in for a treat! With the remainder of the beef, you can make moist and delicious meatballs and meat loaf (both on page 119).

CHEESEBURGERS BEYOND WORDS

6 SERVINGS

1½ pounds chuck roast (ask your butcher to grind it for hamburger)

Healthy pinch of kosher salt

Cracked pepper

6 slices sharp cheddar cheese

6 hamburger buns, white or whole wheat

Bread-and-butter pickles

1 red onion, thinly sliced (optional)

When I lived in New York, there was a restaurant that I went to every Friday night for dinner that served the best cheeseburgers in the whole wide world—cheeseburgers so good that the line out the door would not deter me. The wait was so worth it. Even now, whenever I travel to New York, the first stop I make, right from the airport, is to get a cheeseburger fix, no matter what time it is.

I finally cracked the code as to why these juicy, beefy burgers were so good; all I had to do was ask. The answer was very simple. The cook told me they grind chuck roast fresh every day, fire up the grill really hot, and use kosher salt for flavoring. Sometimes the less you fuss with something, the better. Once you've tried these, you will never go back!

Shape 6 (4-ounce) hamburger patties, each ½ inch thick. Be careful not to pack the meat tightly. You will have dry burgers if the meat is packed too tightly. Sprinkle a healthy pinch of kosher salt over the top of the burger. Crack some pepper over the top as well.

Another secret to great burgers is to get the grill or skillet superhot. Heat the grill pan or cast-iron skillet over high heat for 3 minutes. Place the seasoned side of the burgers on the grill pan. Sprinkle salt and pepper over the top of the burgers. Grill for 2 minutes, then flip the burgers over. Grill for 2 minutes, flip the burgers over again, and grill for 1 minute. Flip the burgers again, and add the cheese on top. Grill for 1 minute more. The burgers will be medium rare. Grill longer if you want your burgers cooked more (medium to well done). Using an instant meat thermometer, test your burgers. Rare beef should be 140°F; well-done beef should be 170°F.

Remove the burgers to a warm plate by the stove (do not cover). Place the hamburger buns on the grill, and toast (on one side only). On a clean plate, assemble the burgers and buns. Use any condiment you like, but I can tell you, these are so tasty that you don't need anything. I do add some bread-and-butter pickles and red onion for the added salt and a crunch, though. You are now ready to bite into the tastiest, juiciest hamburger: so simple, no fuss, just the pure taste of the beef. Enjoy!

POPPI'S MEATBALLS
WITH SAUCE *OR* MEAT LOAF

12 MEATBALLS *OR* 1 MEAT LOAF (4 TO 6 SERVINGS)

The secret to moist and juicy meatballs and meat loaf is to ask your butcher to grind a chuck roast fresh.

Silky Marinara Sauce (page 77)

2 (3-ounce) sweet Italian sausages (optional)

2 pounds freshly ground chuck roast

½ white onion, cut into pieces

1 celery stalk, cut into pieces

1 small carrot, cut into pieces

¼ cup fresh Italian parsley

1 cup bread crumbs

¼ cup grated Parmesan cheese

¼ cup Romano cheese

2 pieces of white bread, crusts removed, torn into shreds

½ cup whole milk

1 garlic clove, crushed through a garlic press

½ teaspoon table salt

1 egg, slightly beaten

¼ cup ketchup

¼ cup olive oil

For Poppi's Meatballs

Prepare the Silky Marinara Sauce.

To make the meatballs *or* the meat loaf, remove the casing from the sausages, and place the sausages in a large bowl along with the ground chuck. In a food processor, pulse to chop the onion, celery, carrot, and parsley until finely chopped. Add the vegetable mixture to the meat. Add the bread crumbs, Parmesan and Romano cheese, white bread, milk, garlic, salt, egg, and ketchup.

Using your hands, mix gently until all of the ingredients are incorporated. Form twelve 4-ounce meatballs (to help you gauge the size, you can use a ¼-inch dry measuring cup). Roll them in your hands to make smooth, round balls. Do not pack them too tightly.

In a saucepan over medium-low heat, bring the marinara sauce to a low simmer.

Heat a frying pan until hot, add the olive oil, and swirl the oil to cover the bottom of the pan. Add the meatballs and brown on all sides; they brown quickly, so watch them to be sure they don't burn. It's not necessary to cook them all the way through; they will finish cooking in the sauce. Carefully lift and place them in the marinara sauce you have prepared, and gently simmer for 30 minutes. Serve with your favorite pasta.

For Meat Loaf

Omit the Silky Marinara Sauce. Prepare the meat mixture as in the meatballs recipe, but shape into a loaf. Place in a 9- by 5-inch loaf pan.

Preheat the oven to 350°F.

Spread ¼ cup ketchup over the top of the loaf. Bake for 60 minutes. Serve with potatoes and Peas with Prosciutto, Tomatoes, and Onions (page 152).

CLASSIC ROAST BEEF

4 TO 6 SERVINGS

1 (3- to 3½-pound) chuck roast, no bone

Kosher salt

Cracked pepper

2 tablespoons canola oil

1 onion, chopped medium

1 carrot, chopped medium

1 celery stalk, chopped medium

2 garlic cloves, minced

2 teaspoons sugar

2 cups chicken stock, homemade (page 52), or store-bought organic chicken broth

1 sprig fresh thyme

¼ cup dry red wine

This is classic roast beef at its finest—so unbelievably moist and tender. The slow roasting for 4 hours allows plenty of time for all the flavors to come together. Over creamy mashed potatoes or polenta is the perfect way to serve this dish.

Preheat the oven to 300°F. Sprinkle the roast generously with the kosher salt and cracked pepper. Heat a Dutch oven or roasting pan with a lid over medium-high heat for 3 minutes. Add the oil and swirl it around the pan. Brown the meat on all sides, 5 to 8 minutes. If the meat starts to smoke, lower the heat. Transfer the meat to a platter.

Over medium heat combine the onion, carrot, and celery in the Dutch oven and cook, stirring occasionally, until they begin to brown slightly. Add the garlic and sugar, and cook for 30 seconds. Add the chicken stock and thyme, and with a wooden spoon, loosen the browned bits of meat that have collected on the bottom and sides of the pot.

Return the roast to the pot, cover, and bring the liquid to a slow simmer over medium heat. Place the pot in the oven and cook for 4 hours, turning after 2 hours.

Transfer the roast to a carving board and place some aluminum foil over the top to keep it warm.

Strain the vegetables and broth, discarding the vegetables. Let the remaining broth settle for 5 minutes; then skim off as much oil as you can. Boil the skimmed broth over high heat, and reduce to about 1½ cups. Add the red wine and continue to boil, again reducing to 1½ cups.

Pull the meat apart into pieces and shreds. Place it back in the pot with broth, and stir to distribute evenly.

Spoon over hot Creamy Yukon Gold Mash with Scallions (page 158) with Caramelized Carrots with Balsamic Syrup (page 156) or peas on the side.

SHORT RIBS
WITH CREAMY POLENTA

6 SERVINGS

Nothing says comfort food better than braised short ribs. The beef turns out tender, moist, and fall-off-the-bone delicious. After hours in the oven absorbing all the succulent flavors of the vegetables, chicken broth, and wine, the beef simply melts in your mouth. My favorite way to serve it is with polenta, but mashed potatoes are just as heavenly.

Preheat the oven to 350°F. Salt and pepper the ribs all over.

Heat a Dutch oven or ovenproof skillet with a lid. Add the canola oil and heat until the oil is hot. Add the ribs, and brown on all sides. Add the red wine, chicken stock, bay leaf, and thyme. Cover and bake in the oven for 3 hours. Remove lid, turn the oven to 450°F, and cook for about 20 or 30 minutes more, basting every 15 minutes, until there are about only 2 cups of liquid left.

Make the polenta according to package directions.

Serve the ribs over the polenta in individual bowls. Spoon pan juices over the top, and garnish with parsley, lemon zest, thyme and chives (if using), a pinch of kosher salt, and fresh cracked pepper.

A few pinches of kosher salt plus additional for sprinkling

½ teaspoon cracked pepper plus additional for sprinkling

6 pounds short ribs, bone in

¼ cup canola oil

2 cups red wine

1 quart chicken stock, homemade (page 52), or store-bought organic chicken broth

1 bay leaf

2 sprigs fresh thyme, plus additional for garnish (optional)

1 (9- to 12-ounce) box quick-cooking polenta

¼ cup fresh Italian parsley, chopped

Zest from 1 lemon

3 tablespoons chopped chives (optional)

GYROS

While in New York, after I've had my hamburger fix from my favorite hamburger hangout, the next thing on my agenda is to stop on the way back to the hotel after the theater to have a gyro. You can smell them a block away grilling up juicy and hot. I love to feel the energy level change in Times Square after the theater has let out and everyone is on such a high from the experience. The mood is intoxicating, as are all the lights and sounds, so what better time is there to enjoy something you love to eat? Gyros are it for me!

Make the Greek salsa first, and set aside. You will have some left over.

In a bowl, combine the lamb, onion, scallion, parsley, mint, mayonnaise, bread crumbs, salt, and cayenne pepper. Using your hands, mix all the ingredients together well. Form 7 to 8 cylinders (about the size of a sausage), 4 inches long and 1 inch wide.

Heat a heavy-bottomed skillet on high heat. Add 2 tablespoons of canola oil and heat until it starts to smoke. Add the lamb, and turn the heat down to medium. Sauté, turning every minute, for about 12 minutes. Remove from the skillet and let rest for 5 minutes before slicing.

Brush the pita bread lightly on both sides with the remainder of the oil. To heat the bread, using tongs, hold each piece over a gas burner set to low, and move it back and forth for 20 seconds on each side, until heated through. Be careful not to burn it. Place the bread on a plate, and cover to keep warm.

To assemble the gyros, slice the lamb into long, ¼-inch-thick slices. Place 2 to 3 tablespoons of tzatziki spread over each piece of warm pita bread. Add a handful of lettuce and ¼ cup of Greek salsa. Place the sliced lamb on top.

Lay a square of foil in front of you on a cutting board with one of the corners at the bottom (so the square looks like a diamond shape). Fold the top half over 3 inches. Place a folded gyro on the foil, leaving 2 inches of foil showing on the bottom. Fold the bottom 2 inches of the foil over the bottom of the gyro. Fold the sides over the gyro, first the left, then the right. You now have a leak-resistant pouch, just like the ones you get from the street vendors in New York. Enjoy!

1 cup Greek Salsa (page 205), or 8 paper-thin slices of red onion and 8 (¼-inch) slices of tomato

1 pound ground lamb

½ medium onion, minced

2 scallions, finely chopped

¼ cup Italian parsley, finely chopped

2 tablespoons finely chopped fresh mint

2 tablespoons low-fat mayonnaise

½ cup panko (Japanese-style bread crumbs)

¼ teaspoon kosher salt

⅛ teaspoon cayenne pepper

4 tablespoons canola oil

4 pieces of Greek pita bread, or 4 pita pockets

2 cups tzatziki spread (page 27)

2 cups shredded iceberg lettuce

4 (9-inch by 9-inch) squares of aluminum foil, set aside

HEARTY BEEF STEW

6 TO 8 SERVINGS

3 pounds chuck roast, cut into
1½-inch pieces

Kosher salt

Pepper

3 ½ tablespoons olive oil

1 cup dry red wine

2 medium yellow onions, chopped
(2 cups)

3 garlic cloves, peeled and minced

2 cups chicken broth, homemade
(page 52), or store-bought organic
chicken broth

1 bay leaf

2 sprigs thyme

2 heaping tablespoons all-purpose
flour

3 (5-ounce) new potatoes or red
potatoes, cut into eighths

3 small carrots, cut into bite-size
chunks

1 cup of peas, fresh or frozen

2 ears fresh corn, kernels cut off
(about 1 cup); you can use canned
or frozen corn instead

Sometimes the tried-and-true dishes are still the best. For me, without question, the ultimate comfort food is a big bowl of hearty beef stew. Serve it with warm, spicy corn bread and a glass of red wine, and I couldn't be happier!

A Dutch oven with a lid is best for this recipe. If you don't have one, use a heavy ovenproof pot with a fitted lid.

Preheat the oven to 350°F.

Season the beef generously with salt and pepper. Heat the Dutch oven on high heat for 2 minutes, until hot; add 1½ tablespoons of the oil and half of the beef. Lower the heat to medium-high. Do not disturb the beef for 2 to 3 minutes. Then, using a large metal spoon, turn the beef; let it cook for 5 minutes more. Transfer the beef to a bowl.

Add another tablespoon of oil to the Dutch oven, and repeat the process with the second half of the beef, but leave the beef in the pot.

Transfer the first batch of meat back into the pot. Add ½ cup of the red wine, and cook until the meat begins to sizzle. Turn off the heat and transfer the meat to a bowl. Set aside.

Over medium heat, add 1 tablespoon of oil into the empty pan. Add the onions and ¼ teaspoon of kosher salt. Stir with a wooden spoon and loosen the browned bits of meat that have collected around the pan. Cook until the onions have become translucent and soft, about 5 minutes. Add the minced garlic and cook for 30 seconds. Add the remaining ½ cup of wine and stir. Add the chicken broth and continue to scrape the edges of the pan. Add the bay leaf and thyme and bring everything to a simmer.

Sprinkle the flour over the top of the beef and mix to coat. Add the meat back into the pot and bring to a simmer again. Cover and put it in the oven for 1 hour. After an hour, remove the pot from the oven and add the potatoes, carrots, peas, and corn. Taste and adjust seasonings as necessary. Place the stew back in the oven for 1 more hour.

GRILLED LAMB CHOPS WITH WHITE NAVY BEAN PUREE

4 SERVINGS

This is another of my go-to dishes when I want to impress my friends for dinner; it's all in the presentation. By placing the perfectly grilled chops on top of the creamy bean puree and adding the finishing touches, you have a dazzling dish that looks so professional. You will be surprised how easy this is to do.

To make the navy bean puree, in a small frying pan, heat the olive oil until hot. Add the garlic and sauté until golden; be careful not to burn it. Discard the garlic, and set the oil aside to cool slightly.

Pour the beans into a food processor, and add the garlic oil, lemon juice, scallion, salt, basil, parsley, and cracked pepper to taste. Process until smooth. Using a spatula, scrape the pureed beans into a bowl, cover, and set aside.

To make the lamb chops, sprinkle kosher salt and fresh cracked pepper as desired on both sides of the chops. Heat an indoor grill pan or cast-iron skillet on high heat until very hot. Pour the olive oil on the grill pan and spread the oil all over the hot grill.

Add the lamb chops, and grill for 2 ½ minutes on each side.

To serve, place 2 heaping tablespoons of bean puree in the middle of each plate. Place the grilled chops on top of the puree, drizzle on balsamic syrup, place a sprig of fresh mint on top, sprinkle on a touch of kosher salt and cracked pepper, and add a fresh lemon wedge on the side.

Navy bean puree

3 tablespoons extra-virgin olive oil

1 garlic clove, smashed

2 (15-ounce) cans navy beans, drained and rinsed

Juice of 1 fresh lemon

1 scallion, chopped

½ teaspoon kosher salt

2 basil leaves

1 tablespoon chopped Italian (flat-leaf) parsley

Cracked pepper

Lamb chops

Kosher salt

Cracked pepper

12 (½-inch-thick) lamb loin chops

1 tablespoon extra-virgin olive oil

Reduced Balsamic Syrup (page 206)

6 sprigs fresh mint

1 lemon, cut into 6 wedges

RACK OF LAMB

6 SERVINGS

Mint syrup

1 cup white wine vinegar

6 tablespoons sugar

½ cup fresh mint leaves

Lamb

2 racks of lamb, 1½ to 1¾ pounds
(7 to 8 chops)

4 tablespoons Dijon mustard

1 teaspoon garlic powder

2 tablespoons low-sodium
soy sauce

1 tablespoon chopped fresh thyme

2 tablespoons extra-virgin olive oil

Lots of cracked pepper

6 small mint sprigs, for garnish

I use to be intimidated by the photographs in cookbooks and magazines of lamb prepared this way. It looked like it was difficult—a lot of work. Well, it is so not! It takes around 30 minutes to make this most impressive dish. It's perfectly seasoned, and the cook time is quick. The meat slices beautifully, is tender and moist, and has a wonderful savory flavor.

You can serve the lamb with a variety of your favorites—garden greens, potatoes, creamy or grilled polenta, or grilled vegetables. My favorite is over baby garden greens with white navy beans and crumbled feta, topped with a sprinkling of pomegranate seeds!

Make the syrup ahead of time, or even the day before. In a saucepan over medium heat, bring the vinegar and sugar to a simmer, cooking until the mixture has the consistency of syrup, 8 to 10 minutes. Continue to cook, reducing by half. Remove the pan from the heat, and let cool for 10 minutes. Add the mint and mix. Cover with plastic wrap and cool for about 1 hour. Store in an airtight container in the pantry, and serve at room temperature.

Preheat the oven to 450°F.

Place the ribs bone side down in a roasting pan. Place 2 tablespoons of the Dijon mustard on each rack of lamb, and rub all over the top with the back of a spoon. Over each rack, sprinkle ½ teaspoon of the garlic powder and drizzle 1 tablespoon of the soy sauce. Divide the thyme over the two racks. Drizzle 1 tablespoon of the olive oil over each rack, and crack plenty of pepper over both.

Bake the lamb for 18 to 25 minutes.

Turn on the broiler. Place the lamb in the broiler 4 inches from the heat source, and broil for 2 to 3 minutes, until the top is golden and bubbly. Keep an eye out so it doesn't burn. Transfer the lamb to a cutting board. Cover lightly with foil and let rest for 5 to 6 minutes.

Slice the racks into chops by cutting between the bones. Place on a platter, or serve 2 to 3 chops per plate, with the mint syrup on the side. Garnish with a sprig of mint (if using). I like to serve White Bean Puree (page 24) with this dish.

LAMB BURGERS OPEN-FACED ON OLIVE BREAD

8 SERVINGS

Sometimes my cravings for hamburgers take on a more challenging taste sensation. That's when I turn to these extremely flavorful and juicy burgers. The ground lamb is seasoned to perfection, and serving the burgers on olive bread with tzatziki, lettuce, and tomatoes gives them a Mediterranean flair. I don't even bother with any sides for these burgers because they're so satisfying and delicious.

Make the tzatziki.

Place the lamb in a large mixing bowl. Add the onion, scallions, parsley, minced mint leaves, garlic, lemon juice, salt, pepper, mayonnaise, and egg yolk. Using your hands, mix until combined. Do not overwork, or the patties will be tough. Form into 8 (4½-inch) patties, each 1 inch thick.

Heat a grill pan or heavy-bottomed skillet over medium-high heat until really hot. Brush both sides of the bread slices with 4 tablespoons of the olive oil. Grill for 1 minute on each side. Set aside.

Pour 2 tablespoons of olive oil into the grill pan and spread it all over the surface of the pan. Add the lamb patties and grill for 4½ minutes on each side. The patties should be slightly pink in the middle. Remove the patties from the grill and let sit for a few minutes while you toss the mesclun.

In a mixing or salad bowl, combine the mesclun and the ½ cup of mint leaves. Add 1 tablespoon of olive oil, the lemon juice, and salt, and toss well.

Place 1 patty on each slice of toast, spoon 2 tablespoons of tzatziki over it, and top with the mesclun.

1 cup tzatziki spread (page 27)

2 pounds ground lamb

¼ cup minced onion

2 scallions, chopped

¼ cup fresh parsley, chopped

½ cup loosely packed whole fresh mint leaves, plus 2 tablespoons minced mint leaves

1 small garlic clove, minced very fine or crushed through a garlic press

3 tablespoons fresh lemon juice

¾ teaspoon kosher salt

Cracked pepper

2 tablespoons low-fat mayonnaise

1 egg yolk

8 slices olive bread

7 tablespoons extra-virgin olive oil

4 cups mesclun salad

2 tablespoons fresh lemon juice

Pinch of salt

OSSO BUCO

6 SERVINGS

Kosher salt

Cracked pepper

4 pounds veal shanks, rinsed and dried

¾ cup all-purpose flour

4 tablespoons olive oil

1 cup dry white wine

4 tablespoons fresh lemon juice

1 quart chicken stock, homemade (page 52), or store-bought organic chicken broth

¼ cup loosely packed Italian parsley, chopped fine

Zest of 1 lemon

This is one of those fall-off-the-bone, melt-in-your-mouth dishes that is truly outstanding. The veal simmers for hours in a combination of wine, lemon, and broth that further tenderizes the meat, and you are left with fork-tender succulent pieces that have been seasoned to perfection. My husband's favorite part is the marrow from the bone shank.

Serve this dish with risotto (page 89) or Creamy Yukon Gold Mash with Scallions (page 158).

Salt and pepper the veal shanks lightly on both sides. Dredge the beef in the flour on all sides.

For 3 minutes, heat a skillet large enough to hold all 4 pieces of beef. Add the oil and swirl it around the pan. Add the beef and sauté for 4 to 5 minutes on each side. Add the wine and cook until the wine is reduced by half. Add the lemon juice and chicken stock. Cover, and bring to just under a boil. Reduce heat to a low simmer. Simmer the meat for 2 hours, turning it after 1 hour.

Remove the lid, raise the heat to medium, and cook until the liquid is reduced to about 1½ cups. The meat is cooked when you can insert a fork easily right through the meat; it should literally be falling off the bone.

Sprinkle on chopped parsley and lemon zest before serving.

COOK'S NOTE: You can also use a beef shank with this recipe and have the same incredible results.

FISH

Going to the market to purchase fish is one of my favorite things to do. I live near the ocean, so it's easy for me to get down to the wharf, where the fresh catch of the day comes in pretty much all day long. I love to watch them unload the trucks with the *frutti di mare* (fruits of the sea) in chopped ice and observe as the fishmongers roll their carts out to prepare the fish for the display case.

I prepare fish at least twice a week. My whole family loves it, and that makes me happy because fish is easy to prepare, low in fat, and versatile. Also, fish such as wild-caught salmon is particularly good for you because it contains high amounts of omega-3 fatty acids and B vitamins.

Fish can be used in salads, pasta, soup, and even sandwiches. I especially love to broil a beautiful piece of cod, halibut, or sea bass and roll it in a corn tortilla with fresh salsa. My favorite way to serve fish, of course, is with a dish of pasta, whether it's in a flavorful bowl of clam sauce seasoned with extra-virgin olive oil, Italian parsley, the perfect amount of garlic, and fresh lemon juice or with plump, juicy sautéed shrimp!

SEA BASS WITH SOY GLAZE AND CUCUMBER SALSA

6 SERVINGS

Cucumber salsa

1 cucumber, peeled, seeded, and chopped

1½ teaspoons low-sodium soy sauce

1 tablespoon rice wine vinegar

2 scallions, chopped

1 tablespoon chopped cilantro

Sauce

¼ cup low-sodium soy sauce

¼ cup mirin

¼ cup sugar

2 tablespoons dry white wine

Fish

6 (3-ounce) sea bass fillets

½ cup all-purpose flour

4 tablespoons olive oil

1 tablespoon sesame seeds

Whenever I want to impress my dinner guests big-time, I make this sea bass with the most wonderful glazed sauce; it's quite impressive. Not only does it make a beautiful presentation served over Creamy Yukon Gold Mash with Scallions (page 158) with the cucumber salsa, but it is also simply beyond-words delicious!

I have to say without hesitation that this is one of my most favorite fish dishes ever. The combination of the creamy mashed potatoes, the delicate fish, and the rich sauce is just perfect.

Make the cucumber salsa first. In a glass bowl, combine cucumber, soy sauce, vinegar, scallions, and cilantro, and mix well. Cover and set aside. You can make the salsa the day before and store in the refrigerator.

To make the sauce, in a medium saucepan over low heat, stir together the soy sauce, mirin, sugar, and wine. Stir frequently until the sugar is completely dissolved, about 3 minutes. Pour the sauce into a small bowl and set aside.

Dredge the sea bass fillets in the flour. Heat a skillet on medium-high until hot. Add the olive oil and heat until hot but not smoking. Sauté the sea bass for 2½ minutes on each side, until browned. Reduce the heat to medium; then pour in the sauce mixture and cover with a lid. Cook until the fish is cooked through, about 5 to 6 minutes.

Place the fillets on a platter, and pour the pan juices over the top. Serve immediately with a sprinkling of sesame seeds and the salsa on the side.

PAN-SEARED CRISPY-SKINNED SALMON WITH GREEN PEA PUREE

4 SERVINGS

8 baby artichokes

2 cups frozen green peas with pearl onions, defrosted

2 ounces low-fat cream cheese

4 tablespoons olive oil

2 leeks, cut into ½-inch rounds and rinsed really well

2 garlic cloves, peeled and smashed

¼ cup white wine

Kosher salt

Cracked pepper

4 (4- to 5-ounce) pieces of salmon, each 2 inches thick

4 tablespoons clarified butter (see Cook's Note on page 156)

¼ cup hot water

8 baby carrots

12 sugar snap peas

3 large shiitake mushrooms, sliced thin (about ½ cup)

8 baby zucchini, sliced on an angle ½ inch thick

1 lemon, sliced thin

This is the recipe I use when I want to impress my guests.

I prepare the salmon by pan searing it in clarified butter, olive oil, salt, and pepper; it's quick and easy. The salmon turns out tender and moist, but my favorite part is the crispy salmon skin.

I serve the salmon over a sweet pea puree with sautéed vegetables on the side, but it can be served in so many ways. Try it over Creamy Yukon Gold Mash with Scallions (page 158), couscous, Caesar salad, spinach salads, or baby greens, or in a Greek salad. It's great in pasta dishes and makes for an outstanding salmon mousse or salmon patties.

With a sharp knife, cut off ½ inch from the top and ¼ inch from the bottom of each baby artichoke. Cut the artichokes in half, and pull off some of the outer leaves. Place the leaves in boiling water for 30 minutes, or until tender, drain, and set aside.

In a blender, combine the peas and onions with the cream cheese, and blend until smooth and creamy, about 2 minutes. Add water a tablespoon at a time if the peas are too thick and the mixture is not blending well. Using a spatula, place the peas in a small sauce pot, and set aside.

Heat a medium-size frying pan over medium-high heat until hot. Add 2 tablespoons olive oil and the leeks, and sauté for 2 minutes. Add the artichoke hearts and garlic, and sauté for 1 minute. Add the wine, and cook until almost all of the wine has evaporated. Cover and set aside.

Sprinkle kosher salt and lots of cracked pepper over the top of the salmon. Heat a frying pan (preferably cast iron) large enough to hold 4 pieces of salmon without overcrowding them (otherwise use 2 skillets) on medium-high heat. Add the clarified butter and remaining 2 tablespoons olive oil, and heat until the oil and butter start to bubble slightly along the edges of the pan. Add the salmon fillets, skin side down, and reduce heat to medium. Cook undisturbed for 4 minutes.

While the fillets are cooking, return the pan with the artichoke hearts back to the stove over medium heat and cook until they begin to sizzle. Add ¼ cup of hot water, the carrots, sugar snap peas, mushrooms, and zucchini. Sprinkle with ½ teaspoon kosher salt, cover, reduce heat to low, and cook for 4 to 5 minutes.

Using a metal spatula, turn the fillets over and sauté for 3 to 4 minutes longer, or until the salmon is just pink in the middle. Flip the fillets gently back onto the skin side, and turn off heat.

Heat the pea puree through on low heat, and stir with a wooden spoon until hot, about 2 to 3 minutes.

To serve, place ¼ cup of the pea puree on each of 4 plates, and top with the salmon, skin side down. Spoon a helping of the vegetables onto each plate, and add a slice of lemon.

POTATO PLATES WITH SMOKED SALMON AND CRÈME FRAÎCHE

6 SERVINGS

1 pound sliced Norwegian or Alaskan smoked salmon

½ cup crème fraîche or low-fat sour cream

3 red potatoes

¼ cup extra-virgin olive oil

3 tablespoons finely chopped red onion (optional)

2 scallions, thinly sliced

3 tablespoons finely chopped Italian parsley (optional)

Freshly cracked pepper

6 lemon or lime wedges

I was experimenting in the kitchen one night with leftover vegetables. I had two red potatoes and thought of making a potato and onion frittata, which I normally would do, but I wanted to try something different.

I looked to see what else was in the fridge and spotted some smoked salmon. Then I remembered how much I absolutely love the salmon pizza at one of my favorite restaurants, Spago, owned by one of my idols, chef Wolfgang Puck. I thought perhaps instead of the pizza dough I could make little plates of potatoes to serve the salmon on.

Though they look complicated and labor-intensive, I promise you they are not! Even I was surprised at how easy they are to make. Now they're a regular in my repertoire.

I served them at a dinner party, and they were a huge hit. They're so pretty to look at on the plate, and they're superdelicious too. You could be polite and cut them with a knife and fork, but I fold mine like a taco; I suggest you tell your guests to do the same!

Preheat oven to 400°F. Let the salmon and crème fraîche sit covered at room temperature on your kitchen counter while you prepare the potatoes.

Thinly slice the potatoes on a mandolin, and lay them individually on a paper towel. Place more paper towels on top and pat dry. It's important to get all of the moisture off the potatoes so they will crisp up nicely in the oven. (You may have more potato slices than needed for the recipe because you'll be using only the best-looking ones.)

Spray a baking sheet with cooking spray. Using 8 potato slices that are pretty much uniform in size, form a flower-shaped circle on the baking sheet: place the first slice on the baking sheet; then place the second slice overlapping half of the first slice. Continue placing slices in a circle, each one overlapping the one before, until you have formed a giant flower. If you need to cover a gap in the flower shape, just add another potato slice. Make 6 potato flowers, brush the potatoes lightly with olive

oil, and bake in the oven for 15 to 20 minutes or until the potatoes are golden crispy. (The middle won't be as crispy as the edges; check to make sure the edges aren't burning. If the potatoes in the back are getting darker than the ones in front, turn your baking sheet around to bake all the potato flowers evenly.) Remove from the oven but leave the potatoes on the baking sheet.

Spread 2 tablespoons of crème fraîche over each potato plate. Add 2 to 3 slices of smoked salmon, and sprinkle on about ¼ teaspoon red onion, or more if you like, 1 teaspoon of scallion, and parsley. Crack some pepper over the top and drizzle with 1 teaspoon of olive oil. Lift each serving gently using a metal spatula, and place on a plate along with a lemon or lime wedge.

COOK'S NOTE: The potato plates can be made in advance and warmed up before you are ready to serve; just place them back in the oven at 400°F for 3 minutes.

ROASTED SHRIMP WITH WHITE BEANS AND SAUTÉED BABY ROMA TOMATOES WITH GARLIC CHIPS

4 TO 6 SERVINGS

Roasting shrimp brings out the sweetness of the fish, which goes beautifully with the smooth, buttery flavor of the beans. This is a great combination of flavors and can be served hot or cold. You can add some wild arugula for a bit of a bite or mix it in with your favorite pasta.

Make the baby Roma tomatoes with garlic chips first.

Preheat the oven to 375°F.

On a baking sheet, arrange the shrimp in one layer. Drizzle olive oil over the top, and add a pinch of kosher salt and lots of cracked black pepper. Mix to coat the shrimp with the oil. Bake for 12 to 15 minutes. Remove from oven, cover lightly with foil, and set aside.

In a cold cast-iron skillet or frying pan, add the pancetta, and turn the heat to medium. Sauté the pancetta until it just starts to turn crispy. Add the sage leaves and sauté until the pancetta is crispy-crunchy. Add the roasted shrimp, and mix. Add the cannellini beans and vinegar and mix gently.

Pour into a serving bowl and add the baby Roma tomatoes with garlic chips over the top. Garnish with the arugula.

Sautéed Baby Roma Tomatoes with Garlic Chips and Capers (page 209), capers omitted

1 pound large shrimp, peeled and deveined

3 tablespoons extra-virgin olive oil

Kosher salt

Cracked black pepper

1 (½-inch-thick) piece pancetta (your deli server can slice you a piece ½ inch thick), cut into small pieces

6 fresh sage leaves

1 (15-ounce) can cannellini beans, rinsed gently and drained

1 tablespoon red wine vinegar

6 cups arugula

CARAMELIZED SCALLOPS WITH WHITE WINE

4 SERVINGS

12 large scallops

Pinch kosher salt

Freshly cracked pepper

4 tablespoons clarified butter
(page 156)

¾ cup white sugar, spread on
a flat plate

½ cup dry white wine

1 fresh lemon, squeezed

1 tablespoon finely chopped
flat Italian parsley

8 chives

1 tablespoon lemon zest

These scallops are tender, sweet, and bursting with flavor. The secret to a beautiful caramelized top is to dip one side of each scallop in sugar and sauté them in clarified butter. Adding white wine with a splash of fresh lemon at the end cuts the sweetness of the sugar. You can cut these scallops with a fork; they melt in your mouth.

The crescent-shaped muscle that attaches the scallop to the shell will toughen when cooked. You need to remove the muscle by peeling it away from the sides of each scallop before cooking. Rinse and dry scallops well. Sprinkle both sides of scallops with a pinch of salt and pepper.

Heat a skillet on medium-high for 2 minutes. Add the clarified butter, and swirl to coat the pan. When the butter starts to foam, get ready to add the scallops. Working quickly, coat one side of each scallop in sugar: hold the sides of the scallop and dip in the sugar, using a twisting motion to coat evenly on one side only. Place the scallops, sugar side down, on the skillet and sauté for 2½ minutes. If the sugar starts to brown too quickly, turn down the heat. Turn the scallops over and sauté for 1 minute. Add the white wine and lemon juice, and reduce by half. After about 1½ minutes, transfer the scallops to a warm platter and pour the pan juices over the top. Garnish with chopped parsley, chives, and lemon zest.

RED SNAPPER
IN RED WINE SAUCE

6 SERVINGS

1 ½ cups flour

1 teaspoon onion powder

1 teaspoon garlic powder

½ teaspoon kosher salt

6 (4- to 5-ounce) red snapper fillets

¼ cup olive oil

4 cloves garlic, peeled and smashed

1 lemon

⅓ cup red wine

1 tablespoon cold unsalted butter, cut into pieces and kept in the refrigerator until ready to use

½ cup Italian parsley, loosely packed and chopped

2 tablespoons capers

You always hear that when you serve fish you should serve it with white wine. I don't know much about wine except that I can appreciate it, but I surmised that it's because fish is delicate and white wine would be a better match.

Once when I was making a fish dish, I didn't have any white wine, so I thought, Well, why not use the red and see what happens? All I can say is, wow! When I used it in this red snapper recipe I was amazed how much the red wine complemented the fish. It was rich and intense in flavor while still being delicate and light.

Sift together flour, onion powder, garlic powder, and salt. Dredge the red snapper in the flour.

Heat a skillet on medium-high for 5 minutes. Add the olive oil and the garlic, and sauté the garlic until golden. Remove the garlic and discard. Add the fish (cook in turns if your pan isn't large enough to hold 6 pieces at once). Sauté the snapper for 2 ½ minutes on one side, turn over, and sauté for an additional 2 ½ minutes. Gently lay all 6 cooked pieces of fish back into the pan. Add the juice from the lemon, then the wine, and cook for 30 to 45 seconds with lid on. Turn off the heat, and let sit for 3 to 4 minutes. Transfer the fish to a warm serving platter, and cover with foil. Add the cold butter a piece at a time to the bottom of the pan. Stir over medium-low heat using a wooden spoon until all the butter has melted. Remove the foil and pour the sauce over the fish. Garnish with chopped parsley and capers.

VEGETABLES

I absolutely love vegetables, and I include them in every meal. I love walking up and down the aisles to look at all the fresh veggies, herbs, and fruits that are available. I make my first pass, observing what is available that day and figuring out how much of what I will need for the next three days. Taking my little rolling shopping cart, I start with the organic lettuce stand and buy baby greens and fresh herbs to flavor my dishes (I like to flavor my dishes using fresh herbs as much as I can, especially when I'm trying to reduce the fat in a dish).

If I find that I don't have the time to stop at the open market, I go to a supermarket that carries organic fruits and vegetables. I eat a lot of fruits and vegetables, and so does my family. I just feel better knowing that they're not consuming pesticides.

I *never* throw away vegetables, even if they are looking a little sad. I put them in a juicer along with fresh fruit for a nutritious pick-me-up or I make a delicious soup! You will be surprised what you can come up with, and you can see my many suggestions throughout the book.

ESCAROLE WITH OLIVE OIL, GARLIC, AND SWEET RAISINS

4 TO 6 SERVINGS

3 ½ pounds escarole, washed

½ cup extra-virgin olive oil

3 garlic cloves, peeled and sliced

½ teaspoon red pepper flakes

¼ cup raisins

2 teaspoons kosher salt

The different flavors in this recipe make for a wonderful surprise—sweet (but not too sweet) and savory with just the right amount of garlic and heat thanks to red pepper flakes, which give it an extra kick!

Not only is this a great side dish for chicken, lamb, or fish, but you can serve it in your favorite pasta, with fresh lemon juice and a generous portion of freshly grated Parmesan cheese. You can mix in grilled or oven-baked sausages; or use it as a topping over fresh baked pizza dough with an extra sprinkle of olive oil, red pepper flakes, and goat cheese.

Place 3 cups of ice in a large bowl, and add 4 cups of water.

Cut 3 inches from the bottom of the escarole, separate the leaves, and rinse under cool water.

In a large pot, bring 4 cups of water to a boil. Add the escarole in batches and cook just until wilted, 5 to 10 seconds. Use tongs to lift the escarole from the boiling water and drop it into the ice bath for a few seconds; then lift it out of the ice bath and into a colander to drain. Continue this process until all the escarole is wilted. You may need to add more ice to the ice bath. Let drain for 10 minutes to get as much water out as you can.

Heat a large, heavy skillet until hot. Add the olive oil, garlic, and red pepper flakes, and sauté until the garlic just starts to turn golden. Add the escarole, raisins, and salt, and mix well to make sure all of the garlic bits are distributed evenly. Cook for 5 more minutes. Serve hot or at room temperature.

PEAS WITH PROSCIUTTO, TOMATOES, AND ONIONS

6 SERVINGS

3 tablespoons olive oil

1 large yellow onion, sliced thin

1 (16-ounce) bag frozen baby peas

3 slices imported prosciutto, chopped

1½ cups chopped tomatoes, fresh or canned

½ teaspoon kosher salt

½ cup water

This has been a traditional recipe in our family for years, and it's so simple to prepare. When I was small, though, I thought this recipe was complicated; when my grandmother prepared it, it seemed like it took forever. Of course, getting those little guys out of their pods took up a lot of time—and guess who was on "peas in the pod" detail? We had a large family, so I had to shell a lot of peas.

After I'd put what looked like a thousand peas in the colander, Nona would just dump them in a pot, smother them with onions, prosciutto, and tomatoes, and turn on the gas. The onions and tomatoes made the peas taste even sweeter, and the prosciutto added the perfect touch of salt.

My daughters Alexandra and Arianna put their own spin on this recipe. Alex makes a delicious creamy pea soup and Ari a fabulous sauce for pasta—so inventive!

Place all the ingredients into a sauce pot over medium heat, cover, and bring to a gentle boil. After 10 minutes, gently mix with a wooden spoon. Cover and continue to gently boil for an additional 30 minutes, checking every 10 minutes to make sure all the water has not evaporated. Add ⅓ cup of water if that is the case. Pour into a serving bowl and serve immediately.

Adjust the seasoning, adding more salt if necessary.

COOK'S NOTE: If you're using fresh peas, shell them, and cook in boiling water for a few minutes until tender. Drain, then follow the recipe as given.

CREAMED SPINACH

8 TO 10 SERVINGS

Creamy spinach with a touch of nutmeg—this is one of the favorite sides I serve for Thanksgiving and often for everyday dinner.

Have all your ingredients ready.

If using frozen spinach, bring 1 cup of water to a boil, and add the frozen spinach. Cover and simmer until the spinach is thawed (about 6 to 8 minutes). Drain in a wire mesh and use a wooden spoon to press as much water as you can out of the spinach.

If using fresh spinach, cook in boiling water just until wilted. Drain. Lay the spinach on a clean dish towel, and spread it out to cool for 30 minutes. Gather all the spinach in the middle of the towel, bring up the sides, and twist tightly, squeezing out as much water as you can. Transfer spinach to a bowl and break apart any clumps. It's important to squeeze out as much water as you can; if too much water is left in, the spinach will be runny and not creamy.

In a sauce pot on medium-high heat, melt the butter. Add flour and mix, forming a roux. Slowly add all of the warm milk, stirring constantly until thickened. Do not boil. The mixture will form tiny bubbles at the edges in 5 to 6 minutes. When that happens, remove from heat, add the salt and nutmeg, and mix well.

Pour the sauce over the spinach, and mix well. Add Parmesan cheese and mix well. Add more salt if necessary.

Preheat the oven to 350°F.

Pour into a baking dish or pie dish and cover tightly with foil. Bake for 30 to 40 minutes.

3 pounds frozen chopped spinach or fresh spinach

4 tablespoons unsalted butter

5 tablespoons flour

4 cups warm milk

1 teaspoon kosher salt

1 teaspoon freshly grated nutmeg

1 cup freshly grated Parmesan cheese

FRENCH GREEN BEANS WITH FETA AND WALNUT-SHALLOT VINAIGRETTE

4 TO 6 SERVINGS

I love my vegetables like I love my pasta: al dente. I want that little crunch in my mouth so I can still taste the freshness of the vegetable. The shallot vinaigrette, along with the saltiness from the feta, the tart of the pomegranate seeds, and the nuttiness of toasted walnuts, adds extra texture and flavor.

3 tablespoons extra-virgin olive oil

1 tablespoon walnut oil

1 tablespoon Dijon mustard

1 tablespoon very finely chopped shallots

1 tablespoon rice wine vinegar

1 tablespoon apple cider vinegar

2 tablespoons lemon juice

½ teaspoon table salt

1 pound French green beans, ends cut or pinched off

Kosher salt

Pepper

½ cup crumbled Greek feta cheese

½ cup toasted chopped walnuts

½ cup pomegranate seeds, in season

To make the vinaigrette, in a medium bowl combine the olive oil, walnut oil, mustard, shallots, rice wine vinegar, apple cider vinegar, and lemon juice. Whisk until smooth and fully combined. Set aside.

Put 3 cups of ice in bowl and fill the rest of the way with cold water.

In a 10-inch frying pan, bring ¾ cup water to a gentle boil. Add the table salt and stir. Add half of the green beans, cover, and boil for 2 minutes. Turn beans with tongs, cover, and boil for 1 more minute. Lift the green beans out of the pan with the tongs and immediately place in the ice water to stop them from cooking. The beans will be a little crunchy in the middle. Cook the remainder of the green beans in the same manner, tossing them in the cold-water bath when through.

Lift the beans out of the water and into a colander to drain. Roll in paper towels to dry. This step is important because if you don't drain all the water off and pat dry the beans well, the dressing will be watered down and the whole dish will taste flat.

If serving immediately, in a salad bowl combine the green beans and the vinaigrette, and toss. Add a pinch of kosher salt and pepper or more, to taste, and toss. Add the feta, walnuts, and pomegranate seeds on top of the beans, and serve.

If you are not serving the green beans right away, cover and refrigerate without the vinaigrette until ready to use. Just before serving, add the vinaigrette to the green beans and gently toss. Adjust the seasoning by adding kosher salt and pepper to taste.

CARAMELIZED CARROTS WITH BALSAMIC SYRUP

4 TO 6 SERVINGS

3 tablespoons clarified butter (see Cook's Note)

2 pounds carrots, sliced diagonally into ½-inch pieces, or baby carrots

1 teaspoon kosher salt

2 tablespoons chopped pecans

Freshly cracked pepper

2 tablespoons Italian parsley, chopped

2 teaspoons Reduced Balsamic Syrup (page 206)

These glazed carrots are fast and easy. The clarified butter is the secret, so be sure to have it ready before you begin. It can be made ahead of time and stored for up to 3 weeks in an airtight container in the refrigerator.

Have all your ingredients ready.

Heat a frying pan on medium-high heat until warm, add the clarified butter, and heat until the butter starts to bubble. Add the carrots and salt. Sauté the carrots until they start to release their juices, about 5 minutes. As you cook the juices down, the natural sugar in the carrots will start to form a glaze and caramelize. Gently turn the carrots over with a metal spatula and continue to sauté, glazing the other side, about 5 to 6 minutes. Do not overcook; the carrots should have a bit of a crunch in the middle.

Add the pecans and sauté for 1 minute. Adjust the seasoning, adding more salt and pepper if necessary. Garnish with chopped parsley and drizzle balsamic syrup over the top.

COOK'S NOTE: To make the clarified butter, in a small saucepan over low heat, melt 1 stick (8 ounces) of unsalted butter, allowing the butter to remain undisturbed. When the butter is melted, carefully remove the foam that forms on top. Pour the clear buttery liquid in a bowl. Be careful not to let the whey at the bottom get into the bowl. Discard the foam and whey. Leftovers can be stored in the refrigerator for up to 3 weeks.

GRILLED ASPARAGUS WITH BALSAMIC SYRUP

4 TO 6 SERVINGS

I prefer the taste of grilled asparagus rather than steamed. Adding balsamic syrup is the perfect finishing touch, providing sweet with a little bit of tart.

Preheat the oven to 450°F. Gently bend the asparagus, and the bottom will snap off naturally at the tough end. Trim with a knife at the breaking point. Rinse and dry completely.

Spread the asparagus out on a baking pan. Drizzle with the olive oil. Using your hands, mix well to coat the asparagus with the oil. Sprinkle ¼ teaspoon salt and ¼ teaspoon pepper over the top.

Bake for about 15 to 20 minutes; the asparagus will be slightly crunchy, not soft. (If you like your vegetables cooked more, leave the asparagus in the oven a little longer.)

Remove from oven and place on platter. Drizzle the balsamic syrup over the asparagus before serving. Sprinkle a pinch of kosher salt and cracked pepper over the top to taste.

2 bunches asparagus
(12 to 14 stalks per bunch)

2 teaspoons extra-virgin olive oil

¼ teaspoon kosher salt plus additional as desired

¼ teaspoon cracked pepper plus additional as desired

2 teaspoons Reduced Balsamic Syrup (page 206)

CREAMY YUKON GOLD MASH WITH SCALLIONS

8 TO 10 SERVINGS

10 (4-inch-long) Yukon gold potatoes, rinsed under cool water

1 cup whole milk, warm

6 tablespoons unsalted butter

2 scallions, chopped

2 teaspoons kosher salt

Cracked pepper

Lemon zest for garnish

I love Yukon gold potatoes. They are creamier and tastier than regular old white potatoes. Don't get me wrong—I love all kinds of potatoes made all kinds of ways, but these are especially good. I use scallions in this recipe just because I like the way the flavors all come together.

Place the potatoes in a large pot and fill with water to cover the potatoes by 2 inches. Bring to a boil; then lower the heat to a gentle boil. Cook until the potatoes are tender, about 30 minutes. Test for doneness by gently inserting a paring knife through the middle. If it goes in smoothly, your potatoes are done. Drain under cool running water and transfer to a bowl. Gently peel off the skins and discard. Run the hot potatoes through a potato ricer over a large pot (the same pot you boiled the potatoes in is fine). (If you don't have a ricer, use a potato masher; the potatoes come out creamier if you use a ricer.) Place the pot on the stove over medium heat and add ½ cup of the warm milk and half of the butter. Mix well until the butter has melted. Add the other ½ cup of milk, the rest of the butter, the scallions (if you are making the potatoes in advance, don't put the scallions in at this point; wait until you are ready to serve), and the salt. Mix well, turning constantly. Taste and add more salt if needed. Serve in a warmed bowl. Add 1 tablespoon of softened butter, if you wish, crack some fresh pepper on top, and sprinkle on lemon zest.

COOK'S NOTE: Since the potatoes take some time to boil, mash, and whip, and then the pots and bowls have to be cleaned, I make my mashed potatoes 4 to 5 hours before I need to serve them. I keep them fluffy and warm by using the double boiler method. I place my mashed potatoes in a ceramic, Pyrex, or stainless-steel bowl on top of a pot filled with water ⅓ of the way up that has been brought to a boil, then turned down to a low simmer. Make sure the pot with the mashed potatoes doesn't sit in the water. It should fit snugly on top of the pot. Keep the potatoes covered. Check the water level every hour or so to make sure there is enough to keep the simmer going. Before you serve the potatoes, use a large spoon to turn the potatoes on the bottom and bring them to the top. If you use this method, add the chopped scallions at the last minute before you serve.

RED POTATOES WITH CLARIFIED BUTTER, ONIONS, AND ROSEMARY

6 SERVINGS (OR DO WHAT I DO—EAT THE WHOLE PLATE YOURSELF!)

12 small red potatoes

⅓ cup clarified butter (page 156)

1 tablespoon fresh rosemary, chopped, or 1 tablespoon dried

6 sprigs fresh thyme; pull about 1 teaspoon of the leaves off to sprinkle over the potatoes while they cook, and save the rest for garnish

1 teaspoon kosher salt

1 teaspoon cracked pepper

1 medium onion, sliced thin

2 tablespoons chopped Italian parsley

These potatoes and onions are so easy to prepare; they make the perfect side dish to any meal, especially if you are a potato and onion lover like me. (I've been known to pick out some of the onions that have crisped up in the pan and eat them right then and there.)

Whenever I make these potatoes and onions, I have to double the recipe; everyone wants seconds!

Rinse and cut the potatoes in half. Dry well with paper towels. Heat a skillet until really hot. Add the clarified butter. When the butter starts to sizzle, add the potatoes, rosemary, thyme, salt, and pepper. Give the skillet a good shake. Cover and reduce heat to medium-low. After 10 minutes, or when the bottoms start to turn golden, flip the potatoes over using a metal spatula. Add the onion, and mix. Cover and cook until the potatoes are soft in the middle and have turned a beautiful golden color and the onions have caramelized, about 30 minutes.

Transfer to a serving dish, and add more salt if necessary. Sprinkle chopped parsley over the potatoes and garnish with a few sprigs of fresh thyme.

SPAGHETTI SQUASH WITH MEATBALLS

4 TO 6 SERVINGS

1 (2- to 3-pound) spaghetti squash

1 teaspoon canola oil

2 ½ teaspoons kosher salt

Poppi's Meatballs with Sauce (page 119)

Freshly grated Parmesan cheese

2 tablespoons chopped fresh basil

Red pepper flakes

My daughter Alex is gluten intolerant, so I make spaghetti squash a lot. She really misses pasta, but she is thrilled that she can add her favorite sauce and get the same kind of enjoyment and satisfaction as if she were eating the real deal.

When I'm trying to watch my carbs, this is a perfect dish to fix. My favorite way to make spaghetti squash is to have it with Poppi's (my dad) meatballs! The squash itself is pretty bland to begin with, but when you add the sauce and meatballs, it's so delicious, you don't miss the pasta at all!

Preheat the oven to 375°F.

Rub the spaghetti squash with canola oil all over, and place it on a baking sheet on the middle rack of the oven. Bake for 1 hour, or until a knife can be inserted all the way through and the squash is tender. Remove from oven and cool for about 45 minutes.

Cut open the squash lengthwise and scrape the seeds out with a fork; discard the seeds. Slide a fork along the inside of the squash from top to bottom to release the strands. You will see they will look like long pieces of spaghetti.

Place the strands in a baking dish, add salt, and mix well. Spread 2 ladlefuls of sauce on top to cover the squash. Sprinkle liberally with freshly grated Parmesan cheese, cover with foil, and bake at 350°F for 25 minutes.

Heat the rest of the sauce together with the meatballs on low heat for about 6 to 8 minutes to make sure the meatballs are hot and the sauce is heated through.

Serve individual portions in heated pasta bowls with extra sauce and at least 2 meatballs per serving. Garnish with Parmesan cheese, basil, red pepper flakes, and kosher salt to taste.

GRILLED VEGGIES

6 TO 8 SERVINGS

1 bunch asparagus (about 12 to 14 stalks), rinsed and bottoms snapped off

2 zucchini, sliced on a diagonal ¼ inch thick

4 Japanese eggplant, sliced on a diagonal into ¼-inch-thick pieces

2 red bell peppers, seeded and cut into quarters

1 large yellow or red onion, peeled and sliced into round ¼-inch pieces

3 tablespoons extra-virgin olive oil

Reduced Balsamic Syrup (page 206)

Kosher salt

Fresh oregano, for garnish

I grill up vegetables on my indoor grill pan almost every night. It's easy and fast, and the results are so delicious—not to mention healthy.

I like to make more than I need because I use the leftovers for grilled panini sandwiches or vegetable burritos, chopped up with salads, or tossed into a pasta dish.

Preheat an indoor or outdoor grill pan until hot. Brush the vegetables with olive oil all over using a pastry brush (you can use any combination of vegetables you like). Add the vegetables to the hot grill in batches, and keep an eye on them, since some veggies grill up quicker than others.

Arrange the grilled vegetables on a platter, and drizzle extra olive oil and reduced balsamic syrup over the top. Finish with a sprinkle of French or kosher salt and fresh oregano. Serve hot, cold, or at room temperature.

BLACK BEAN CHEESEBURGER

6 SERVINGS

There's always at least one vegetarian in the group, so I make these tasty and oh-so-good burgers made with beans. When they're served on toasted whole wheat buns with all the condiments, you don't miss the meat at all!

This is also a great way to save on your grocery bill. You get the protein you need, and it cuts down on fat and cholesterol too! I've served these to my family and guests often, and they think they're genius.

In a mixing bowl, combine the beans, scallions, red bell pepper, mustard, jalapeño, salt, and egg yolk. With your hands or a fork, squish the beans until all the ingredients are incorporated. You are not making a smooth paste; you want to see some of the whole beans mixed in. Cover with plastic wrap and put the mixture in the refrigerator for 45 minutes. Shape the cold bean mixture into hamburger patties. They will be sticky and a bit loose. Handle gently.

Heat a cast-iron skillet until hot. Add the oil. When the oil is hot enough (you can test by putting one bean in; if it starts to sizzle, you're good to go), lift the burgers one at a time with a spatula, and slide them into the pan, spaced 1 inch apart. Sauté for 2 minutes. Turn over carefully and sauté for 2 more minutes. If they start to fall apart on the sides, just gently press them back using the spatula. While the patties are cooking, start to toast the hamburger buns. Turn the patties over once more, and add the cheese. Cover and continue to cook for 1 minute, allowing the cheese to melt.

Place the patties on buns and add the condiments.

2 (15-ounce) cans black beans, drained and rinsed well

2 scallions, finely chopped

½ red bell pepper, chopped into tiny pieces

1 tablespoon Dijon mustard

1 jalapeño, chopped into tiny pieces (optional)

½ teaspoon kosher salt

1 egg yolk

¼ cup canola oil

6 whole wheat hamburger buns

6 slices of sharp cheddar cheese, or Monterey jack cheese

Lettuce, tomato, pickles, mustard, and ketchup, for garnish (optional)

Guacamole (page 19), for garnish

Tomato Salsa (page 217), for garnish

DESSERTS

I was born without a sweet tooth. Desserts were never my thing. Frankly, I was and still am intimidated by baking. Baking takes time, thought, and precise measuring, all the things that take up too much time and for which I have no patience. When I cook a meal, I don't use measuring spoons or cups. My hands are my measuring spoons, and I eyeball everything else, and that's not good if you want cakes to rise, frostings to spread smoothly, piecrusts to be flaky, and cookies to be crisp and chewy.

I have over the years tried my hand at baking, only to become frustrated over the fact that I suck at it. I make too much of a mess, get flour over everything, don't have enough measuring cups or spoons so I'm constantly cleaning them out for the next ingredient, and then freak out because I find out that I'm out of baking soda so I have to rummage through the refrigerator to find the open box of soda that keeps my fridge free of odors. After I finally get everything mixed together, I remember that I didn't grease and flour the cake pans and I forgot to preheat the oven. Instead of calling it a dessert, I call it a disaster. Yes, I actually ask my family what they would like for disaster. One day I finally decided to do something about it. I called a professional cooking school and took a baking course along with my daughter Arianna, who loves baking. I was determined to conquer my fear of measuring.

READ BEFORE BAKING

Baking is a science, and if you follow the simple rules (although I didn't know how simple the rules really were until I stopped fighting it), you will have amazing success. It still takes time and precision, especially measuring. Once you apply the rules and understand why molecules need their environment to move around in order for them to do their thing, why you mix wet ingredients into dry, why butter and eggs should be at room temperature for cakes and chilled for pies, along with other simple rules, you will have amazing results.

The secret here is patience, a preheated oven, and everything measured out and ready to go beforehand, referred to in the culinary world (I learned this in class) as *mise en place*, a French phrase that means "put in place." I'm proud to say that Arianna and I received our graduation certificates, and I now have a chef's jacket with my name embroidered on it from the cooking school.

I enjoy baking now so much, and even though I still don't have a sweet tooth, I love baking for my family and friends. Following are some simple tips and suggestions to make your baking experience more enjoyable and successful too.

Before You Start to Bake

+ Have your oven checked out to make sure it is properly calibrated.
+ If the oven is too hot or not hot enough, I promise you, you will not be happy with the results.
+ Remember to preheat your oven before you start to bake.
+ Read the whole recipe before you start baking.
+ Have all of your ingredients measured out and lined up.

If You Are Baking a Cake

+ Grease the bottom of the cake pan first with butter; this will help the parchment paper stay put.
+ Line the cake pan with parchment paper cut into rounds to fit.
+ Grease the top of the parchment paper.
+ Coat the bottom and sides of the pan with 2 tablespoons of flour. Tap the pan on the counter to release excess flour, and discard.

Use of Butter in Cakes

To cream butter is to beat tiny air bubbles into it that will result in a light cake. Let the butter sit at room temperature right from the refrigerator for 30 minutes before mixing. Lightly poke the butter with your finger. Your finger should be able to make a dent in the butter but should not be able to go through the whole stick. There should be some light resistance. Creaming the butter with sugar is a very important step to ensure a light and airy cake. You should mix the butter and sugar until the mixture has increased in volume and turned a pale yellow, for 3 to 4 minutes. Stop at least twice during creaming to scrape the sides of the mixing bowl.

Use of Butter in Pies

The use of butter in a piecrust makes all the difference if you want a tender, flaky crust. I like to use European-style butter because it's richer and creamier, has a high fat content, and is tastier and easier to work with. The temperature of the butter or fat and the water is crucial to a flaky crust. The butter should be cold and the water ice cold to ensure a flaky crust. I place the cold butter in the freezer for 10 minutes before cutting it into small cubes. Refrigerate the dough before you roll it out.

Eggs

Eggs should be at room temperature and added into batter slowly, one at a time, to help them to emulsify, which is important for the texture of the cake. If you add all the eggs at one time, the cake will lose volume and will not be as light.

If you are whipping egg whites, it's important to whip them at room temperature. You will get more air and therefore more volume, which is important if you are making meringue or a soufflé.

Measuring Flour and Sugar

I was surprised to learn on my very first day of baking class that I was measuring my flour all wrong. I always scooped the flour from the bag with a measuring cup and leveled it off with a knife, then poured it in the mixing bowl. Wrong! My cakes always came out with puffy domes, or too dry or too dense. The culprit is excess flour in the batter, which absorbs way too much liquid and makes the batter heavy.

Prepared batter needs to go into the oven immediately; if you wait too long, you will end up with a cake that won't rise or a cake that falls in the middle.

The best way to measure dry ingredients is to spoon the flour into a dry measuring cup (rather than dipping the cup into the flour), and never pack the flour down. Drag a knife sideways across the top of the measuring cup to get rid of excess flour.

I find that when I measure my dry ingredients this way, instead of dipping a measuring cup into them, my results are amazing.

Note: Remember that when you are measuring by volume, there is a difference between 1 cup of flour, sifted, and 1 cup of sifted flour, so read your recipes carefully.

Mixing Wet and Dry Ingredients

Add the liquid ingredients to the dry ingredients in stages, as this will prevent the formation of gluten in the flour. Your cake will end up tender and moist. Make sure you follow the method suggested in the recipe for the best results.

CARROT CAKE WITH CREAM CHEESE FROSTING

10 TO 12 SERVINGS

This carrot cake is thick, rich, and delicious. A great cup of coffee, tea, or ice-cold milk (my personal favorite), along with a great book, my husband, a warm blanket, and music, and I'm so happy. What more do you need? This a true guilty pleasure.

Adjust the oven racks to the center of the oven. Preheat the oven to 350°F. To prepare the pans, butter the bottom and sides of 2 (9-inch) cake pans. Line the bottoms with parchment paper and butter the top of the paper. Add 1 tablespoon of flour on top of the parchment in each cake pan, and shake the pan back and forth to dust the bottoms and the sides of the pans. Then tap the cake pans on the side of the counter to get out the excess flour; discard the flour.

To make the cake, sift together the 2 cups of flour, baking soda, baking powder, cinnamon, nutmeg, and salt into a mixing bowl for a mixer fitted with a paddle. Add the sugar, oil, eggs, carrots, coconut, walnuts, and raisins. Mix just until blended. Do not overmix. Divide the cake batter between the two cake pans, and bake for 50 minutes or until a toothpick inserted into the cake comes out clean. Cool the cakes for 5 minutes; then use a butter knife to loosen the cakes from the sides of the cake pans. Turn over onto a cooling rack, and let rest until completely cool.

To make the creamy cream cheese frosting, combine the cream cheese and butter in a mixer fitted with a paddle, and mix together for 1 minute. Add the sour cream and mix. Add the confectioners' sugar and vanilla, and whip until creamy smooth.

To frost the cake, cover the top of one layer of the cake with a thick layer of frosting. Place the second cake layer on top, and use the rest of the frosting to cover the top and sides of the whole cake. If desired, use a cake decorator with a tip that makes pretty floral designs to embellish the top of the cake. Sprinkle sliced almonds, chopped pecans, or walnuts over the top, if desired, for a professional-looking cake.

To prepare the pans

Unsalted butter

2 tablespoons flour

Carrot cake

2 cups unbleached all-purpose flour

1½ teaspoons baking soda

2 teaspoons baking powder

1½ teaspoons ground cinnamon

½ teaspoon grated nutmeg

1¼ teaspoons salt

1¾ cups granulated sugar

1½ cups canola oil or safflower oil

4 large eggs, at room temperature, slightly beaten

6 medium carrots, rinsed, peeled, and grated on a box grater (this should yield about 2 cups)

½ cup flaked coconut

¾ cup chopped walnuts

½ cup raisins

Cream cheese frosting

8 ounces (2 packages) cream cheese, softened

8 tablespoons unsalted butter (1 stick), at room temperature

1 tablespoon sour cream

2¼ cups confectioners' sugar

1 teaspoon vanilla

½ to 1 cup sliced almonds, chopped pecans, or walnuts, to sprinkle over the cake

CHEESECAKE WITH FRESH BERRIES

10 TO 12 SERVINGS

Graham cracker crust

1½ cups graham cracker crumbs

¼ cup sugar

¼ teaspoon cinnamon

⅓ cup plus 2 tablespoons unsalted butter, melted

Filling

3 (8-ounce) packages cream cheese, at room temperature

1 cup sugar

3 large eggs, at room temperature

½ cup sour cream, at room temperature

2 tablespoons lemon juice

1 tablespoon vanilla extract

1¼ cups sour cream, at room temperature

3 tablespoons sugar

Topping

2 pints fresh raspberries or strawberries; if using strawberries, slice in half and lay flat on top of cake.

I love to put fresh strawberries, raspberries, or blueberries on top of this cake; it looks so beautiful and makes an impressive presentation. Keep the cheesecake in the refrigerator until ready to serve to keep the berries from running, as they have a tendency to release their juices. In fact, I usually put the berries on at the last minute or no more than 2 hours before I am ready to serve to keep that from happening.

Preheat the oven to 325°F.

To make the crust, in a medium-size bowl stir together the graham cracker crumbs, sugar, cinnamon, and butter until moistened. Using your hands, press the crumbs into the bottom of a 10-inch by 3-inch springform pan. Bake for 15 minutes, and cool completely.

To make the filling, in a mixer using the paddle attachment, mix the cream cheese for two minutes, stopping twice to scrape down the sides of the bowl. Add 1 cup of sugar in an even stream, and mix for 2 more minutes, until light and fluffy. Remember to stop at least twice to scrape down the sides of the bowl. Add the eggs one at a time, processing after each addition to incorporate thoroughly, and scrape down the bowl each time. Add the ½ cup of sour cream, lemon juice, and vanilla. Process until well blended. Scrape down the sides of the bowl. Pour the filling into the crust, and spread evenly in the pan. Lift the pan and tap it on the counter several times to release any bubbles in the batter. Bake for 1 hour, or until the top is set. Use a toothpick; if it comes out clean, the cake is done. If it still wiggles in the middle, you need to bake it more. Do not overbake.

While the cheesecake is baking, combine the 1¼ cups sour cream and 3 tablespoons sugar. Spread this mixture over the cheesecake immediately after removing it from the oven. Return the cake to the oven for 5 minutes to set. Cool completely on a wire rack; then cover with aluminum foil and freeze overnight.

Take the cheesecake out of the freezer the morning you are going to serve it. After 1 hour, release and remove the pan sides. Top with berries and serve.

PUMPKIN CHEESECAKE

10 TO 12 SERVINGS

Crust

9 whole graham crackers

12 gingersnap cookies

½ cup chopped pecans

2 tablespoons sugar

½ teaspoon ground ginger

½ teaspoon ground cinnamon

6 tablespoons unsalted butter, melted

Filling

3 (8-ounce) packages of cream cheese, at room temperature, cut into chunks

1¼ cups sugar

1 teaspoon ground cinnamon

½ teaspoon ground ginger

¼ teaspoon freshly grated nutmeg

¼ teaspoon ground cloves

½ teaspoon salt

5 large eggs, at room temperature

1 cup heavy cream

1 (15-ounce) can plain pumpkin

1 tablespoon vanilla extract

1 tablespoon fresh lemon juice

This is the perfect cheesecake for the holidays, and I always end up making two because this is the first dessert to go. When it's baking, you can smell the aroma of the cinnamon and spices all over the house. It's a beautiful dessert too, with its rich, creamy texture and deep golden color. Add a dollop of fresh whipped cream, if you like, and drizzle your favorite store-bought caramel sauce over and serve with spiced hot tea. It tastes like Christmas.

Preheat the oven to 325°F. Put an oven rack in the lower-middle part of the oven. Spray a 9-inch springform pan with nonstick cooking spray.

To make the crust, in a food processor, combine the graham crackers, gingersnap cookies, pecans, sugar, ginger, and cinnamon. Process until evenly ground. Add the melted butter and process for 5 to 8 seconds. Turn the crumbs into the prepared springform pan, and spread the crumbs into an even layer using your hands and pressing gently. Bake for 15 minutes. Cool on a wire rack to room temperature, about 30 minutes. When the crust is cool, wrap the outside of the pan with two 18-inch square pieces of foil, and set the springform pan in a roasting pan.

To make the filling, in a food processor, process the cream cheese, sugar, cinnamon, ginger, nutmeg, cloves, and salt until smooth. Add the eggs one at a time, processing after each addition. Add the cream and pumpkin, and process until well blended. Add the vanilla and lemon juice. Pour the filling into the crust, and spread evenly. Tap the pan on the counter 4 to 5 times to remove air bubbles.

Place the cheesecake in the roasting pan, and place the roasting pan in the oven. Quickly fill the roasting pan with water halfway. Bake for 1 hour and 15 minutes, or until the top is set. To test, insert a toothpick; if it comes out clean, the cake is done. Remove the cheesecake from the water bath, and place it on the counter to cool to room temperature. Refrigerate overnight.

To release the cake from the springform pan, run a knife under warm water, and run the knife all around the cheesecake to loosen the sides. Release the sides of the springform, and gently lift it away from the cake. Slice and serve with fresh whipped cream.

PHYLLO CUPS WITH GREEK YOGURT, FRESH PEACHES, AND HONEY

6 SERVINGS

Butter-flavored cooking spray

1 (3½-ounce) package
phyllo dough

½ cup Greek yogurt

3 medium ripe fresh peaches,
pitted, skinned, and cut into
1-inch pieces

¾ teaspoon ground cinnamon

2 tablespoons chopped walnuts

12 small fresh mint leaves

2 tablespoons honey

This is a very versatile dessert because you can use any kind of fruit you prefer in the recipe. I make mine with Greek yogurt and fresh peaches, but you can substitute your favorite ice cream, frozen yogurt, or sorbet.

Preheat the oven to 375°F. Spray a 6-cup muffin tin generously with cooking spray.

Remove 6 sheets of phyllo from the package, and cover them with a kitchen towel to keep them from drying out. Store the rest of the phyllo in the refrigerator.

Lay 1 sheet of phyllo dough on a work surface, and keep the remaining sheets covered with a damp towel to prevent them from drying out. Spray the sheet lightly with cooking spray. Cut the sheet into 5 (6-inch by 6-inch) squares. Place 1 square gently inside a muffin cup, and press the bottom to fit into the cup. Lay the other 4 squares in the muffin cup at different angles until all 5 have been gently pressed in. The ends of the phyllo dough will be taller than the cup and should overlap. Repeat the process for the other 5 muffin cups.

Bake for 5 to 8 minutes or until golden brown. Remove from the oven and let cool completely before trying to lift the cups from the muffin tins. Gently lift the phyllo cups and place on a platter. Fill each to the top with yogurt. Add half a peach, and sprinkle with ⅛ teaspoon of cinnamon, 1 teaspoon of chopped walnuts, 2 mint leaves torn into small pieces, and 1 teaspoon of honey.

MELON MEDLEY WITH LEMON SORBET, COOL AND REFRESHING

6 SERVINGS

In the summer, there is nothing more satisfying than melons at the peak of flavor. I can eat melons all day long—and I do! I love to mix my melons together and serve them for breakfast, snacks, and desserts. I often eat cut-up melons with creamy Greek yogurt and a drizzle of honey over the top for breakfast. I also like to puree it with ice, fresh orange juice, and frozen yogurt to make a great fruit smoothie. Kids love it!

Here is a recipe for a light and refreshing snack or dessert that's very simple.

Cut up all the melons with a melon baller and place in a glass bowl. Add the orange juice, and mix well. Sprinkle with fresh mint, and mix. Cover and chill in the refrigerator for 1 hour. Serve with lemon, lime, or orange sorbet or your favorite fruit sorbet. Frozen vanilla yogurt also works well.

3 cups seedless watermelon

1 ripe cantaloupe, cut in half and seeded

1 crenshaw melon, cut in half and seeded

2 cups fresh orange juice

½ cup fresh mint

6 scoops lemon, lime, or orange sorbet

STRAWBERRY SHORTCAKE

4 TO 6 SERVINGS

Strawberry coulis and whipped cream

2 quarts fresh strawberries, hulled, washed, and sliced

1 cup fresh orange juice

1 cup sugar

1 tablespoon cornstarch

¼ cup water

2 cups heavy whipping cream, whipped

1 teaspoon vanilla extract

Shortcake

1 ¾ cups all-purpose flour

1 tablespoon baking powder

½ teaspoon salt

3 tablespoons sugar

½ stick (4 tablespoons) cold unsalted butter, cubed (keep in the refrigerator until ready to use)

½ cup heavy cream

⅓ cup plain yogurt

2 quarts fresh strawberries, hulled, washed, and sliced

1 tablespoon lemon or orange zest

10 to 12 fresh mint leaves

When strawberries are in season, this is my family's favorite dessert. Here are a few suggestions for tender shortcakes. First, make sure your butter is cold (after I've cubed the butter, I like to stick it in the freezer for 5 minutes). Second, don't overwork the butter into the dry ingredients. Third, after adding the wet ingredients into the dry, mix just until the dough has come together (you will have a tough cake if you handle the dough too much). Finally, when you use the cookie cutter, do not twist it into the dough (twisting seals the edges, and the cake will have trouble rising; you want your shortcakes to be high, fluffy, and flaky).

The coulis can be made 3 days ahead. To make the coulis, in a saucepan combine the sliced strawberries, orange juice, and sugar. Bring to a boil, and continue to cook until the sugar has melted, about 5 minutes. Strain through a wire mesh into a saucepan. Mix the cornstarch and water together until smooth. Heat the strained strawberries over medium heat. Add the cornstarch mixture and stir until slightly thickened. Remove from heat and let cool to room temperature. Pour into an airtight container and place in the refrigerator to chill (the coulis should be served cold).

To make the whipped cream, combine the whipping cream and vanilla in the mixing bowl of a mixer fitted with a wire whisk. Whip until stiff peaks form. Cover with plastic wrap and refrigerate until ready to use.

To make the shortcakes, have all of the ingredients ready. Preheat the oven to 425°F. Line a baking sheet with parchment paper.

In a bowl, whisk together the flour, baking powder, salt, and sugar. Cut the butter into the flour mixture using a pastry blender, and keep cutting until the butter is the size of small peas.

Whisk the cream and yogurt together. Add it to the flour mixture and blend with a fork until the dough comes together. Do not overmix or the dough will be tough. Pat the dough out on a lightly floured surface into a 1-inch-thick rectangle. Using a 2 ½- or 3-inch round cookie cutter, cut (do not twist) as many shortcakes as you can from the rectangle. Place

the shortcakes on the baking sheet. Gently press the scraps together and cut out more shortcakes. Bake for 15 to 20 minutes. Remove from the oven and let cool for 10 minutes.

When ready to serve, slice the shortcakes in half horizontally. On the bottom half, pile on as many fresh sliced strawberries as you like. Pour 4 to 5 tablespoons of strawberry coulis over the top of the strawberries, sprinkle with ½ teaspoon lemon or orange zest, add a dollop of whip cream and some fresh mint, and top with the other half of the shortcake.

COOK'S NOTE: You can use these shortcakes with blueberries, raspberries, and fresh summer peaches too.

BROWNIES,
RICH AND CHOCOLATY

12 BROWNIES (OR MORE IF YOU SLICE SMALLER)

½ cup unsalted butter cut into cubes, at room temperature, plus additional for greasing the pan

3 ounces unsweetened chocolate, chopped

1 cup sugar

⅛ teaspoon salt

2 large eggs, slightly beaten, at room temperature

1½ teaspoons vanilla extract

¾ cup cake flour

1 cup semisweet chocolate chips

½ cup walnuts, chopped (optional)

In my quest to achieve the best results from my recipes, I experiment until I come up with dishes that I am completely in love with. I experimented with these brownies until I literally couldn't stand the smell or taste of chocolate anymore (I'm okay now).

I don't like brownies that are cakey, too dense, too intense, chewy, or dry. After many, many attempts, I have come up with the perfect combo—enjoy.

Preheat the oven to 350°F. Grease an 8-inch square baking dish with butter. Line the dish with parchment paper cut to fit the pan, and grease the top of the parchment paper.

In a saucepan on low heat, combine the ½ cup butter and unsweetened chocolate. Cook, stirring often, until all of the chocolate has melted. Stir in the sugar and salt. Remove from heat and let cool for 10 minutes. Add the eggs and vanilla and mix, blending well. Add the flour and mix just until blended. Add the semisweet chocolate chips and walnuts and mix to combine. Don't overmix.

Pour the batter into the prepared baking dish and spread evenly. Tap the dish on the counter three or four times to get rid of any bubbles in the batter and to further even it.

Bake the brownies until a toothpick inserted into the center comes out almost clean, about 30 minutes. Do not overbake. Let cool on a wire rack for 30 minutes. Using a butter knife, gently loosen the sides of the brownie from the baking dish. Invert the baking dish over a plate large enough to hold the brownies, and release them from the dish. Remove the parchment paper. Let cool completely before slicing into squares.

CHOCOLATE VALENTINE FROM THE HEART

10 TO 12 SLICES

You don't have to wait for Valentine's Day to enjoy this smooth, rich, creamy, decadent piece of heaven. When you serve this bit of chocolate heaven, slice off a small portion—not your ordinary slice of cake, because it's very potent, so be careful; a little goes a long way. I wash it down with an ice-cold glass of milk or on a chilly night with a cup of hot tea or a steamy latte.

Preheat the oven to 350°F. Place a rack in the middle of the oven. Place a roasting pan large enough to hold the cake while it's baking on the middle rack (you are going to bake this cake in a water bath). Fill the pan almost halfway up with hot water.

Grease the bottom and the sides of a 9-inch heart-shaped baking pan. Place the baking pan on a piece of parchment paper and trace around the bottom with a pencil. Cut the heart shape out of the parchment and place inside the pan. Grease the top of the parchment paper.

To make the cake, bring a small amount of water to a simmer in a pot that you will use as the bottom of a double boiler. Combine the chocolate and water in a stainless-steel bowl small enough to fit in the pot but large enough that it does not touch the simmering water. Place the bowl over the rim of the pot, and stir frequently until the chocolate is completely melted and smooth. Remove the bowl from the heat, set aside, and allow to cool.

In a stainless-steel bowl small enough to fit in the pot with the simmering water but large enough that it does not touch the water, whisk together the eggs, sugar, and salt until blended. Set the bowl over the pot with the simmering water to warm the eggs, for about 1 minute. Whisk constantly; you want to just warm the eggs. Be careful not to let the water touch the bottom of the bowl—you don't want to make scrambled eggs!

Transfer the egg mixture to a mixing bowl. Using a wire whisk attachment, beat at high speed until the mixture has tripled in volume (about 3 minutes).

Cake

9 ounces bittersweet chocolate, chopped

⅓ cup water

5 eggs, at room temperature

1 cup granulated sugar

¼ teaspoon salt

⅔ cup whipping cream

Bittersweet chocolate glaze

9 ounces bittersweet chocolate, coarsely chopped

1 cup heavy cream

1 teaspoon vanilla

In the meantime, using a hand mixer whip the heavy cream until firm and peaks just start to form. Gently fold the cooled chocolate into the eggs completely; then fold in the whipped cream.

Pour the batter into the prepared cake pan, and place the pan in the prepared hot-water bath. Bake for 40 to 50 minutes, or until a toothpick inserted in the center comes out clean.

Transfer the pan to a wire rack, and let it cool for 25 minutes. Invert the cake onto the wire rack, remove the pan, and gently peel off the parchment paper. Let the cake cool completely; then, using a metal spatula, carefully and gently transfer it from the cooling rack to a plate. Cover with plastic wrap, and place it in the refrigerator for at least 2 hours.

To make the glaze, place the chocolate in a food processor and process until finely ground. Pour the chocolate into a ceramic bowl. In a small saucepan, bring the cream to a boil. Pour the hot cream over the chocolate and stir until the chocolate is melted and the mixture is smooth. If necessary, place the ceramic bowl over a pan of simmering water to further melt the chocolate and bring the mixture to a smooth and creamy consistency. Add the vanilla and stir.

When you're ready to glaze the cake, lift it off the plate gently and place it on a wire rack over a baking sheet. Pour the warm glaze over the top of the cake, and spread it evenly all over the top and sides with a knife or rubber spatula, covering the cake completely. The excess chocolate will drip onto the baking sheet. Let the cake set for 10 minutes. Using a metal spatula, transfer from the wire rack to a cake plate. Press whole pecans around the outside, or sprinkle chopped nuts over the top and drizzle on your favorite chocolate sauce.

FLOURLESS CHOCOLATE CAKE

8 TO 10 SERVINGS

This cake is insanely delicious and extremely rich, smooth, and extra chocolaty—a chocolate lover's dream!

Use half of the 1½ tablespoons of butter to grease the inside of an 8- or 9-inch round cake pan. Line the pan with parchment paper; grease the paper with the other half of the 1½ tablespoons of butter. Dust with the cocoa powder.

In the top of a double boiler over simmering water, combine the chocolate and ¾ cup of butter, and melt completely. Mix together well and set aside to cool, about 20 to 30 minutes.

Using a mixer with a wire whisk on medium-high, beat the egg yolks, ¼ cup of the sugar, 1 tablespoon of the coffee, the vanilla, and the salt for 3 minutes, until the mixture is pale and thick. With the mixer on medium-low, slowly add the cooled chocolate mixture; beat until well incorporated.

In a clean bowl, beat the egg whites using the wire whisk until foamy. Gradually add the 2 tablespoons of sugar, beating until medium-firm peaks form. Gently fold half of the egg whites into the chocolate mixture. Fold in the remaining egg whites just until no streaks remain.

Preheat the oven to 300°F. Spread the batter in the pan. Bake for 40 minutes, until the cake puffs slightly and a toothpick inserted into the center comes out moist. Do not overbake. Cool on a rack for 30 minutes.

Run a butter knife around the inside of the pan to loosen the cake; then invert it onto a flat plate. Gently lift off the pan and peel off the paper. Cool at room temperature for 1 hour; refrigerate for 3 to 4 hours.

To make the glaze, combine the butter and chocolate in a double boiler over simmering water and melt, whisking until smooth. Whisk in the corn syrup until the glaze is smooth and shiny. Set the cake on a wire rack over a large baking sheet. Pour the warm glaze over the center of the cake. The glaze should cover the surface evenly, spilling over the edges and down the sides, with all the excess falling onto the baking sheet. Refrigerate for 2 hours, or until firm.

Slice the cake in small slices (it's very rich), dipping your knife into hot water and wiping it dry before you cut each slice.

Chocolate cake

¾ cup (12 tablespoons) unsalted butter cut up into pieces plus 1½ tablespoons unsalted butter for greasing the pan

2 tablespoons unsweetened cocoa powder

10 ounces bittersweet chocolate, finely chopped

5 large egg yolks, at room temperature (set 3 egg whites aside; save the other 2 for an egg-white omelet)

¼ cup plus 2 tablespoons sugar

1 tablespoon instant espresso, dissolved in ½ cup hot water

1 teaspoon vanilla

Pinch of salt

Chocolate glaze

½ cup (8 tablespoons) unsalted butter, cut into pieces

8 ounces bittersweet chocolate, chopped into small pieces

2 tablespoons light corn syrup

SUPER-DUPER DOUBLE CHOCOLATE CHIP COOKIES

ABOUT 2 DOZEN COOKIES

2¼ cups all-purpose flour

1 teaspoon baking soda

½ teaspoon salt

1 cup (2 sticks) unsalted butter, at room temperature

¾ cup sugar

¾ cup brown sugar, firmly packed

1 teaspoon vanilla extract

2 eggs, at room temperature

4 cups semisweet chocolate morsels

1½ cups chopped walnuts or pecans

1 cup raisins

I like to save the dough for these cookies in plastic egg cartons. Instead of throwing the cartons away, I thoroughly wash them in soap and water, and then I use them to hold my golf ball–size scoops of cookie dough. I can stack the cartons in the freezer without taking up too much room.

This is an easy way to share these treats, and do your part to recycle, too. You can wrap pretty ribbons around the cartons and give them out as gifts. I also use them as party favors. When my guests leave, they leave with homemade cookie dough they can bake up themselves, fresh from the oven.

Preheat the oven to 325°F. Line a cookie sheet with parchment paper to fit the pan.

In a medium bowl, mix the flour, baking soda, and salt.

With an electric mixer using the paddle attachment, beat the butter and sugars for 2 minutes, until fluffy. Scrape down the sides of the bowl with a spatula, add the vanilla, and beat for 1 minute. Scrape the sides of the bowl again. Beat in the eggs one at a time until well incorporated. Scrape down the sides of the bowl after each addition. Slowly add the flour mixture, and mix until blended. Add the chocolate morsels, nuts, and raisins, and mix well.

Using a small ice cream scoop, place golf ball–size pieces of cookie dough on the cookie sheet. Don't worry if you crowd them at this point, they need to be chilled first before they're baked. Chill for 1 hour in the refrigerator.

When ready to bake, line another cookie sheet with parchment paper. Place the chilled cookie dough balls at least 3½ inches apart on the cookie sheet, and bake in batches. Bake for 30 minutes, or until the cookies are golden-brown on top. Keep your eye on them; check them after 15 minutes. Using a metal spatula, place the cookies on a rack to cool. (I can only wait 10 minutes; then I go for it—while the chocolate is still melty—with a cold glass of milk.)

FOURTH-GENERATION RICE PUDDING

12 TO 14 SERVINGS

My husband's family has had this recipe in their family for generations. His dad ran a Greek diner in the Bronx, and people used to come from miles around to eat this creamy rice pudding. This is a true feel-good food.

I've served it for every family holiday meal, for Sunday meals, and for no reason at all—other than everyone loves it.

In a heavy 4-quart pot, combine the milk and heavy cream. Bring the mixture just to a boil over medium-high heat (small bubbles will appear around the edge of the pan), stirring frequently. Stir in the rice, sugar, raisins, and butter. Bring the mixture to a boil again; then reduce the heat. Cover and simmer, stirring frequently, until the rice is tender, about 1 hour. Beat the eggs in a bowl until light. Temper the eggs by combining ¼ cup of the cooked rice mixture with the eggs, stirring quickly. Add the egg-rice mixture back into the pot and incorporate with the rest of the rice. Stir constantly over low heat until the pudding thickens, about 3 minutes. Remove from the heat.

Serve nice and hot right out of the pot, or keep covered and cool before serving. Spoon the pudding into dessert dishes and sprinkle with cinnamon.

The pudding will keep in an airtight container in the refrigerator for 3 days. I love it cold right out of the fridge.

7 cups whole milk

2 cups heavy cream

1 ⅓ cups long grain rice

1 cup sugar

¾ cup raisins

¼ cup unsalted butter

3 large eggs

1 teaspoon ground cinnamon, for garnish

BLACKBERRY COBBLER

4 TO 6 SERVINGS

Filling

6 cups blackberries

⅓ cup sugar

1 tablespoon all-purpose flour

2 teaspoons lemon zest

Pinch of salt

Topping

1 ¼ cups all-purpose flour

⅓ cup sugar

2 teaspoons baking powder

½ teaspoon ground cinnamon

¼ teaspoon salt

1 large egg yolk, beaten,
at room temperature

½ cup buttermilk

6 tablespoons unsalted butter,
melted

½ teaspoon pure vanilla extract

Fresh mint, for garnish (optional)

I love to make cobblers. They're easy to do, and you can make most of them with your favorite fruit. Big juicy blackberries are my choice, and in a cobbler warm and sweet, there is nothing better!

Preheat the oven to 375°F. Lightly grease a glass pie plate.

To make the filling, in a large bowl, gently toss the blackberries with the sugar, flour, lemon zest, and salt in a large bowl until blended. Pour into the prepared baking dish and set aside.

For the topping, stir together the flour, sugar, baking powder, cinnamon, and salt in a large bowl. In another bowl, whisk together the egg yolk, buttermilk, butter, and vanilla, blending well. Pour the wet ingredients into the dry ingredients. Using a rubber spatula, fold gently until the flour is moistened and the mixture forms a soft dough.

Drop heaping spoonfuls of the topping onto the fruit filling, spacing them evenly over the surface. Don't worry if the topping doesn't cover all of the fruit.

Bake until a toothpick inserted into the topping comes out clean, about 45 minutes. The fruit should be bubbling and the top browned.

Serve warm, at room temperature, or right out of the refrigerator with a scoop of vanilla ice cream or frozen yogurt and a sprinkling of fresh mint (if using).

PEACH CRUMBLE

6 TO 8 SERVINGS

Filling

6 ripe (not mushy) large
yellow peaches

⅓ cup packed dark brown sugar

1 tablespoon fresh lemon juice

1 tablespoon fresh lemon zest

½ teaspoon ground cinnamon

1 teaspoon cornstarch

Topping and garnish

1½ cups all-purpose flour

¾ cup granulated sugar

¾ cup light brown sugar

1 cup oatmeal

½ cup walnuts

¼ teaspoon kosher salt

½ pound (2 sticks) cold
unsalted butter, diced

Peaches are without a doubt my very favorite food in the whole world. There is nothing better than a perfectly ripe peach. When peach season is at its height, usually mid-August, I eat peaches every day, almost all day long. The season is so short, so I savor every one.

I also like to mix peaches in my Greek yogurt with cinnamon and a twist of lemon. I slice them up to have with my oatmeal, and cut them up to put in my cereal, on salads, and in pies and smoothies. My grandfather used to cut them up and put them in his wine; he always let me have some. (Boy, did I like that!) He's the one who gave me this recipe for Peach Crumble. I've been making it forever to serve my family, and it's so good.

Adjust the oven rack to the lower-middle of the oven.

Slice the peaches in half and remove the pit. Peel off the skin. Using a knife or a melon baller, scoop out and discard the red flesh from the pit area. Into a bowl, slice the peaches into ¾- to 1-inch slices. Add the sugar, lemon juice, lemon zest, and cinnamon. Toss gently. Let sit for 20 minutes.

Drain the peaches into a colander over another bowl, saving the juice. Return the peaches to the original bowl.

To the juice add the cornstarch, and whisk to get rid of the lumps. Pour over the sliced peaches and gently mix well. Pour into a 12-inch by 8-inch shallow baking dish.

Preheat the oven to 400°F.

To make the topping, combine the flour, granulated sugar, brown sugar, oatmeal, walnuts, salt, and butter in the bowl of an electric mixer fitted with the paddle attachment.

Mix on low speed until the mixture is crumbly and the butter is the size of peas. Scatter the topping evenly all over the peaches.

Bake for 40 to 50 minutes, until the peaches bubble and the top is browned.

Serve warm or at room temperature with ice cream or frozen yogurt.

FRESH FIGS WITH PORT WINE AND BALSAMIC GLAZE

6 SERVINGS

You can use this same recipe with several dishes. Try it in a salad of baby greens served with Stilton or blue cheese, with thinly sliced prosciutto and burrata cheese for an appetizer, or for a surprisingly different dessert with vanilla ice cream and drizzled with balsamic glaze.

Heat a frying pan on medium heat. Add the oil and butter. When the butter has melted, add the figs, cut side down, and brown, without disturbing them, until they have started to caramelize, about 4 to 5 minutes. Turn one over gently with a metal spatula to see if the fig is a deep golden color on the bottom. If not, continue to sauté. When the figs have caramelized, add the port and cook down until a syrup forms.

Divide the figs among 6 individual dessert plates.

Add 1 to 2 tablespoons of water to the frying pan, and stir up the syrup on the bottom of the pan. Mix well and pour over the tops of the figs. Drizzle balsamic syrup over the top, and sprinkle with mint, lemon zest, a pinch of kosher salt, and the toasted chopped pecans. Serve warm, cold, or at room temperature with a scoop of French vanilla ice cream or vanilla frozen yogurt on the side.

1 tablespoon olive oil

1 tablespoon unsalted butter

12 fresh figs, cut in half

¼ cup port wine

1 to 2 tablespoons water

Reduced Balsamic Syrup (page 206)

1 tablespoon fresh mint, finely chopped

2 teaspoons lemon zest

Pinch of kosher salt

3 tablespoons chopped pecans, toasted (optional)

COOK'S NOTE: To toast the pecans, place them in a small cold frying pan on medium heat. Warm them until they start to release their oil and turn golden, about 2 to 3 minutes. Be careful not to burn.

DRESSINGS, SAUCES, AND SALSAS

Salad dressing enhances the flavor of any salad. It's important not to use too much dressing when preparing your fresh greens, though. Too much will overpower their earthy flavor and can even wilt them. I like to use fresh herbs and flavored oils such as garlic-infused olive oil, walnut oil, pistachio oil, and hazelnut oil, to name just a few. Flavored vinegars such as aged balsamic, red and white, raspberry, and my favorite, champagne, add the perfect acidity and balance to your dressing. You can savor the taste of all these wonderful dressings without losing the fresh qualities and crispness of your big, beautiful bowl of salad!

It's important to mix your salad and eat it right away. Leaving your salad to sit for more than 5 minutes with the dressing on, especially if you salted it, will give you one big bowl of blah. The salt will wilt your lettuce in a matter of seconds, releasing water and leaving you with a soggy salad. Don't be afraid to use the salt, however; it does bring out the flavor of your salad and keep it from tasting bland. If I'm serving a buffet, I mix the salad at the last minute and call everyone to the table to come and enjoy!

SHALLOT VINAIGRETTE

1 CUP

1 tablespoon Dijon mustard

1 tablespoon finely chopped shallot

¾ cup extra-virgin olive oil

2 tablespoons rice wine vinegar

1 tablespoon apple cider vinegar

2 tablespoons fresh lemon juice

1 teaspoon kosher salt

This is my favorite vinaigrette. It goes great with all kinds of salads as well as vegetables. Try this on your next potato salad instead of mayonnaise.

Combine the mustard and shallot in a bowl, and whisk in the olive oil slowly. Continue to whisk to incorporate all the ingredients until smooth. Add the rice wine vinegar, apple cider vinegar, and lemon juice. Whisk to blend all ingredients until smooth. Add salt. This vinaigrette will keep in an airtight container for up to a week in the refrigerator.

HERBED VINAIGRETTE

¾ CUP

½ cup extra-virgin olive oil

1 tablespoon Dijon mustard

¼ cup fresh lemon juice

2 tablespoons minced shallot

1 tablespoon minced fresh oregano leaves

¼ teaspoon kosher salt

Cracked pepper

2 tablespoons chopped fresh Italian parsley

5 fresh basil leaves, chopped

1 garlic clove, peeled and smashed

I enjoy the flavor of fresh herbs infused into salad dressings. Try some of this Herbed Vinaigrette over grilled fish.

Whisk the olive oil with the Dijon mustard until incorporated. Slowly add the lemon juice, then the shallot, oregano, salt, pepper, parsley, and basil leaves, and whisk well. Add the garlic. Store in the refrigerator in an airtight container until ready to use. Make sure to whisk the dressing again before you use it. It will last for up to 4 days in the refrigerator.

ASIAN SLAW VINAIGRETTE

¾ CUP

This is a great dressing for slaw because its hearty and potent flavor stands up to crunchy shredded cabbage. I like to use this vinaigrette as a dipping sauce for steamed Chinese dumplings.

In a food processor, combine the soy sauce, lime juice, brown sugar, chili pepper, cilantro, gingerroot, and molasses. With the machine running slowly, drizzle in the peanut oil and olive oil until the mixture is blended. It will be thick, creamy, and homogenized. This vinaigrette will keep in the refrigerator for 3 days in an airtight container.

2 tablespoons low-sodium soy sauce

2 tablespoons fresh lime juice

¼ cup dark brown sugar

1 serrano chili pepper, chopped

2 tablespoons chopped fresh cilantro

1 tablespoon minced fresh gingerroot

1 tablespoon dark molasses

¼ cup peanut oil

¼ cup extra-virgin olive oil

CHAMPAGNE VINAIGRETTE

ABOUT ⅓ CUP

¼ cup extra-virgin olive oil

1 tablespoon Dijon mustard

2 tablespoons champagne vinegar

1 small garlic clove, smashed

1 teaspoon minced shallot

⅛ teaspoon kosher salt

Cracked pepper

The first time I tasted a dressing that had champagne vinegar in it, I remember my reaction. I noticed a clean, fresh, slightly sweet flavor. I just loved it and starting using champagne vinegar for dressings. Although I use all the dressings in this chapter, I have to say that this recipe and the shallot vinaigrette are at the top of my list!

Whisk together the olive oil, Dijon mustard, and champagne vinegar until emulsified. Add the garlic, shallot, and salt, and stir. Add pepper to taste. Place in an airtight container and let sit for at least an hour. This dressing will keep in the refrigerator for 4 days in an airtight container.

RASPBERRY VINAIGRETTE

ABOUT ¾ CUP

½ cup extra-virgin olive oil

2 tablespoons walnut oil

1 teaspoon finely chopped shallots

2 tablespoons rice wine vinegar

1 tablespoon malt vinegar

1 tablespoon raspberry vinegar

¼ teaspoon kosher salt

This very light, summery-tasting dressing is especially great on fresh fruit such as raspberries, peaches, cantaloupe, and, yes, even watermelon! Toss these fruits into your salad. You'll be surprised at how good it is!

In a glass bowl, combine all of the ingredients and whisk together well. Store in an airtight container in the refrigerator for up to 3 days.

HOMEMADE CROUTONS

4 CUPS

12 slices sourdough bread, cut into 1-inch cubes

3 tablespoons olive oil

2 teaspoons garlic powder

2 teaspoons onion powder

½ teaspoon kosher salt

I prefer to make my own croutons; it's easy to do, and they taste so much better than store-bought. The extra-virgin olive oil helps give them a deep golden color and extra flavor. Take that extra step and make the croutons yourself; you will definitely see and taste the difference.

Preheat the oven to 350°F.

Place the cubed sourdough bread in a large bowl. Drizzle the olive oil on top and, using your hands, mix well.

Combine the garlic powder, onion powder, and salt in a bowl, and mix well. Sprinkle over the bread, and mix well.

Spread the seasoned bread out on a baking sheet, and bake until the cubes are dried, golden, and crunchy, 30 minutes or more.

Store in an airtight container in the pantry for up to 1 month.

PROSCIUTTO BITS

½ CUP

12 slices imported prosciutto

I use prosciutto bits in salads, on top of thick and hearty soups, and over eggs and omelets to add a little salty crunch.

Preheat the oven to 350°F.

Place the prosciutto slices in one layer on a baking sheet, and bake for 20 to 30 minutes, or until the prosciutto is crisp. Remove from the oven and let cool.

Chop into small bits. Keep in an airtight container for up to a week in your pantry.

CUCUMBER AVOCADO SALSA

1½ TO 2 CUPS

This salsa is cool and refreshing, and the jalapeño gives it just the right amount of heat. It's great with crudités and over grilled meats, chicken, and fish!

Combine all of the ingredients in a bowl, and toss gently to combine.

If not using within 10 minutes, cover immediately with plastic wrap and place in the refrigerator for no more than 1 day, until ready to use.

2 ripe avocados, peeled, seeded, and cut into ½-inch pieces

1 hot house or English cucumber, seeded and diced (about 2 cups)

2 tablespoons fresh lime juice

½ teaspoon kosher salt, plus additional if desired

1 small jalapeño, seeded and chopped

2 tablespoons finely chopped cilantro leaves

¼ cup chopped red bell pepper

GREEK SALSA

3 TO 4 CUPS

My Gyros recipe (page 125) is the best with this salsa, but this salsa is so good on a beautiful grilled T-bone steak as well. Grilled shrimp or chicken is perfect with it too. The sweetness of the baby tomatoes comes right through, and it's all brought to life by the red onion and fresh flavor of the oregano.

Stir the tomatoes, cucumber, red onion, olive oil, lemon juice, vinegar, oregano, and pepper to taste together in a bowl. Let stand at room temperature until ready to serve. Just before you serve, add the salt. If you put the salt in too early, it will extract the juices from the vegetables and will make the salsa runny. Add the crumbled feta cheese. Store in an airtight container in the refrigerator for up to 3 days.

COOK'S NOTE: You can substitute blue cheese for the feta.

2 quarts baby Roma tomatoes or cherry tomatoes, cut in half lengthwise

1 medium cucumber, seeded, skin on, diced into small pieces

2 tablespoons diced red onion

2 tablespoons extra-virgin olive oil

2 teaspoons fresh lemon juice

1 tablespoon red wine vinegar

2 teaspoons chopped fresh oregano

Cracked pepper

¼ teaspoon kosher salt

4 ounces Greek feta cheese, crumbled

BLUE CHEESE DRESSING

ABOUT 1 ½ CUPS

⅔ cup buttermilk

1 cup sour cream

2 tablespoons champagne vinegar

6 ounces blue cheese

⅛ teaspoon cayenne pepper

My husband Tony's favorite salad is a cold crisp wedge of head lettuce with chopped heirloom tomatoes, onions, and prosciutto bits, with this creamy blue cheese dressing on top.

Whisk together the buttermilk and sour cream until smooth. Add the vinegar and whisk in. Break the blue cheese into pieces and fold into the buttermilk mixture. Sprinkle the cayenne over the top, and mix.

Cover tightly. This dressing will keep in the refrigerator for 3 days.

REDUCED BALSAMIC SYRUP

½ CUP

1 (16.9-fluid-ounce) bottle balsamic vinegar

I use reduced balsamic vinegar (which I also call balsamic glaze) on almost everything I serve, including ice cream!

Its sweet-tart flavor is the perfect finishing touch to many dishes. Whenever I'm in doubt and I feel a recipe calls for an extra kick of added flavor, I just bring out my needle-nose bottle of balsamic syrup and create extra magic!

Pour the whole bottle into a small saucepan and bring to a boil over high heat. Lower heat to medium-high and continue to boil until the vinegar starts to thicken and forms a syruplike consistency, about 15 to 20 minutes. Be careful not to thicken too much, or you will end up with a thick black goop. To test, use a wooden spoon: if the syrup coats the back of the spoon, it is ready to remove from the heat. Let it cool to room temperature before you store it in the refrigerator. I use a needle-nose plastic bottle to store my glaze after it has cooled. It will last up to 2 months in the refrigerator.

BALSAMIC DIJON VINAIGRETTE

ABOUT ¾ CUP

Balsamic vinegar is rich in flavor, and you can't miss it when it's mixed in a salad. This is one of my favorites for when I'm serving crudités. You just want to use a spoon, not a sliced vegetable, to eat it!

In a bowl, whisk the mustard, shallot, and salt. Add the olive oil, and whisk until the oil is incorporated into the mustard. Add the rice wine vinegar, sherry wine vinegar, and balsamic vinegar. This vinaigrette will keep in the refrigerator in an airtight container for up to 4 days.

1 tablespoon Dijon mustard

1 shallot, minced fine

¼ teaspoon kosher salt

½ cup extra-virgin olive oil

1 tablespoon rice wine vinegar

1 tablespoon sherry wine vinegar

3 tablespoons balsamic vinegar

SAUTÉED BABY ROMA TOMATOES WITH GARLIC CHIPS AND CAPERS

2 ½ TO 3 CUPS

Have you any idea how wonderfully delicious these baby Romas are on focaccia bread, on crostini, grilled fish, chicken, steak, or even tossed in pasta? Take my word for it: they're outstanding—hot or cold. Even grilled and roasted vegetables taste better with this on top or mixed in.

Heat a frying pan until hot. Add the olive oil. Add the garlic, and sauté until the garlic turns slightly golden. Quickly add the tomatoes, and sauté for 2 to 3 minutes. Add the salt and red pepper flakes, mix, and remove from the stove. Add the capers and parsley. Store in an airtight container in the refrigerator for up to 1 week.

5 tablespoons olive oil

2 garlic cloves, thinly sliced

2 cups baby red Roma tomatoes

2 cups baby yellow Roma tomatoes

2 teaspoons kosher salt

⅛ teaspoon red pepper flakes

2 tablespoons capers

¼ cup loosely packed Italian parsley, finely chopped

GINGER DIPPING SAUCE

¾ CUP

1 tablespoon warm water

1½ tablespoons sugar

5 tablespoons seasoned
wine vinegar

½ cup low-sodium soy sauce

1 tablespoon sesame oil

1 teaspoon Sriracha chili sauce
(you can find it in the Asian section
of your market)

2 tablespoons minced fresh ginger

1 small garlic clove, minced

6 thin slices seeded jalapeño

8 cilantro leaves

This is my go-to dipping sauce when I want to serve steamed dumplings or spring rolls that I picked up in the frozen food section of the market to make my life easier. It makes for an easy and quick appetizer when I'm pressed for time or when I just want to just kick back and don't feel like preparing a whole meal. This dipping sauce is spectacular with grilled shrimp as well.

Mix together the water and sugar, and stir until sugar dissolves.

In a small bowl whisk together the vinegar, soy sauce, sesame oil, chili sauce, and sugar water. Stir in the ginger and garlic. Add the jalapeño and cilantro, and mix.

Use right away, or refrigerate for up to 2 days in an airtight container.

AVOCADO DIPPING SAUCE

3 TO 3½ CUPS

3 tablespoons lime juice

1 tablespoon Tabasco sauce

1 teaspoon cumin

¾ teaspoon kosher salt

2 tablespoons chopped white onion

2 large avocados, peeled, pitted,
and cut into chunks

1 cup low-fat sour cream

This is a perfect dipping sauce for a great big platter of fresh vegetables. Believe it or not, this is a big hit on game day in our house.

Place all of the ingredients in a food processor, and process until smooth and creamy. Adjust the seasoning, adding more salt if you like.

PONZU DIPPING SAUCE

1¾ CUPS

This is a great dipping sauce for boiled shrimp, grilled fish, and fresh vegetables, especially thinly sliced cucumbers.

Combine all of the ingredients in a bowl, and mix well. This sauce can be stored in an airtight container in the refrigerator for up to 3 weeks.

¼ cup low-sodium soy sauce

½ cup mirin

½ cup fresh lemon juice

½ cup sugar

1 scallion, minced

SPICY SOY DIPPING SAUCE

ABOUT ½ CUP

This is a great sauce for dipping egg rolls, steamed or fried dumplings, or fried shrimp. It can enhance the flavor of grilled vegetables too; just brush them with the sauce before grilling.

Mix all of the ingredients together. This sauce can be stored in an airtight container in the refrigerator for up to 2 weeks.

⅓ cup low-sodium soy sauce

1 tablespoon sesame oil

¼ cup balsamic vinegar

2 teaspoons chili garlic sauce

LIME AND CUMIN VINAIGRETTE

¾ CUP

I like to use this vinaigrette as a marinade for beef, shrimp, and chicken, as well as a great dressing for Chinese chicken salad and boiled baby potatoes.

Place all of the ingredients in a bowl and stir well. This vinaigrette will keep in the refrigerator in an airtight container for 2 days.

½ cup extra-virgin olive oil

¼ cup fresh lime juice

½ teaspoon cumin

¼ teaspoon salt

¼ teaspoon cracked pepper

2 tablespoons finely chopped fresh cilantro

2 tablespoons finely chopped fresh basil

2 tablespoons finely chopped fresh mint

GREEN GODDESS

1 CUP

I normally do not like creamy dressings; for me they're just too heavy on lettuce. This dressing is light, with a tang and a bit of spice that wake up your taste buds.

Place all of the ingredients in a blender, and blend until creamy smooth. This dressing will keep in the refrigerator for 3 days in an airtight container.

¾ cup buttermilk

1 ripe avocado, peeled and seeded

3 tablespoons white wine vinegar

1 teaspoon coarsely chopped tarragon

1 scallion, minced

Pinch of cayenne

MANGO SALSA

5 TO 5½ CUPS

I really love fruit salsas. I serve this one to liven up grilled or sautéed fish; it brings out a sweet and tangy flavor that serves as a perfect complement.

Place all of the ingredients in a glass bowl, and mix. Cover with plastic wrap, and chill for at least an hour to allow the flavors to combine. Garnish with a few slices of jalapeño just before serving. This salsa can be served chilled or at room temperature. Store in an airtight container in the refrigerator for up to 3 days.

2 cups small chunks fresh pineapple

2 cups small chunks fresh mangos

1 cucumber, peeled, seeded, and cut into small chunks

2 tablespoons finely chopped red onion

1 tablespoon seeded and finely chopped jalapeño, plus a few slices of jalapeño for garnish

½ teaspoon kosher salt

Cracked pepper

1 cup cilantro, loosely chopped

2 tablespoons fresh lime juice

1 tablespoon fresh lemon juice

2 tablespoons extra-virgin olive oil

GREEN APPLE CHILI SALSA

1 CUP

Try this salsa on your next cole slaw salad. Serve with sandwiches and in sandwiches for a wonderful crunchy delight in every bite!

Combine all the ingredients in a bowl (cracked pepper to taste), and mix well. Cover with plastic wrap, and refrigerate for at least 1 hour. Store in an airtight container in the refrigerator for up to 3 days.

1 Granny Smith apple, diced small

1 scallion, chopped

2 tablespoons small-dice red onion

¼ cup diced red bell pepper

2 tablespoons chopped cilantro

2 tablespoons apple juice

1 tablespoon extra-virgin olive oil

1 tablespoon red wine vinegar

1 tablespoon lime juice

⅛ teaspoon chili powder

Pinch of kosher salt

Cracked pepper

1 tablespoon diced jalapeño (optional)

TOMATO SALSA

2 CUPS

This versatile salsa can be used as a topping over eggs, grilled meats, or fish or as a dip with tostada chips.

Bring 8 cups of water to a boil. Lop off the top portions of the tomatoes and place them in the boiling water for 30 seconds. Using a slotted spoon, lift the tomatoes from the boiling water and into a bowl. Immediately run them under cool water to peel the skins.

The skins should come off easily. If not, place back into the water for another 15 to 20 seconds.

Cut the skinned tomatoes in half lengthwise, and remove the core and seeds using a paring knife. Discard the skins, cores, and seeds.

Dice the seeded tomatoes into small pieces.

Place the tomatoes, red onion, cilantro, scallions, lime juice, salt, jalapeño, and olive oil in a glass bowl, and mix well. Cover in an airtight glass container and place in the refrigerator for at least 3 to 4 hours before serving. This salsa can be made the day before and will last 3 to 4 days in the refrigerator in an airtight container.

8 Roma tomatoes, peeled, seeded, and diced into small chunks (about 2 cups)

½ cup red onion, chopped small

¼ cup cilantro loosely packed, then finely chopped

2 scallions, finely chopped

2 tablespoons fresh lime juice

1 teaspoon kosher salt

1 tablespoon jalapeño, finely diced with the seeds (optional)

1 tablespoon olive oil

SALSA VERDE

½ CUP

My daughter Alex makes this salsa verde a lot and puts it on everything, even her toast! It's packed with flavor, so a little goes a long way.
I spread salsa verde on bread for sandwiches instead of mayonnaise, ketchup, or mustard.

Place all of the ingredients in a glass bowl and mix. Cover and let sit for 1 hour. Store in an airtight container in the refrigerator for up to 3 days.

3 tablespoons finely chopped shallots

1 tablespoon chopped mint

1 cup packed Italian parsley, chopped

2 anchovy fillets, chopped

8 pitted green olives, finely chopped

2 tablespoons capers, rinsed and chopped

4 tablespoons extra-virgin olive oil

4 tablespoons white wine vinegar

PANTRY AND STAPLE ITEMS

It's so important to keep a well-stocked pantry and a few staple items in your refrigerator at all times. There's nothing worse than preparing a recipe and realizing halfway through that you are missing an important ingredient—it could be something as simple as an egg, salt, or oil.

If you keep a well-stocked pantry and staple items readily available, it will save you time, money, and the aggravation of getting into your car to go and get the one item you're missing. That has happened to me one too many times in the past. Inevitably I would get stuck in a long line at the checkout counter while I anxiously waited behind people who were just as anxious as I was to get home. I would start to get a little fidgety when someone paid by check and then had to go fishing in his or her wallet for a driver's license that was simply not to be found. I would keep reminding myself that if only I would remember to keep my pantry items in check, I wouldn't have to go through this.

Having a well-stocked pantry also comes in handy when you forget to stop at the market or are just too spent to even think about making dinner. Some of my favorite resources are the Cheese Store of Beverly Hills, Williams-Sonoma, Gelson's, the Santa Monica Farmer's Market, and Whole Foods Market.

Lists of pantry and staple "must haves" begin on page 220.

TEN ESSENTIAL ITEMS

If you keep these ten essential items in your kitchen, you're ready to make a meal at any time, whether you've been to the grocery store or not!

1. Extra-virgin olive oil

2. Fresh lemons, at least 6

3. Kosher salt

4. 1 quart chicken broth, homemade or canned

5. 1 (15-ounce) can cannellini beans

6. Low-sodium soy sauce

7. 1 bunch of scallions

8. 1 (28-ounce) can chopped tomatoes

9. 1 jar Dijon mustard

10. 1 bulb fresh garlic

MUST-HAVE PANTRY ITEMS

These items will come in handy, especially on busy nights—or when unexpected guests arrive. You'll have everything you need to prepare a fabulous meal and enjoy your company, too.

Oil

- Extra-virgin olive oil
- Canola oil
- Peanut oil
- Sesame oil
- Vegetable oil
- Cooking spray

Vinegars and Sauces

- Apple cider vinegar
- Balsamic vinegar
- Seasoned rice wine vinegar
- White wine vinegar
- Mirin (you can find it in the Asian section of your market)
- Low-sodium soy sauce
- Salsa
- 28 ounces of enchilada sauce

Condiments and Spices

- Dijon mustard
- Yellow mustard
- Grainy mustard
- Mayonnaise
- 1 bottle of ketchup
- 1 bottle of Tabasco sauce
- 1 box of kosher salt
- 1 box of table salt
- Black peppercorns
- Red pepper flakes

Stocks and Broths

- 2 quarts of organic chicken stock
- 2 quarts of vegetable stock
- 1 to 2 quarts of homemade chicken stock

Vegetables

- 2 (28-ounce) cans of chopped tomatoes
- 2 (28-ounce) cans of tomato puree
- 2 cans or tubes of tomato paste
- 2 (15-ounce) cans each of cannellini beans, white navy beans, black beans, garbanzo beans, baked beans
- 16 ounces of dried green peas
- 2 cans of nonfat refried beans
- 2 cans of corn
- 1 bottle of capers

Grains and Pastas

- 1 tube of polenta
- 1 (16-ounce) package each of assorted semolina pasta (angel hair, linguine, penne, farfalle, pastina, couscous)
- 1 box of Arborio rice (for risotto)
- Brown rice
- Panko (Japanese-style bread crumbs)

- Bread crumbs
- Bread (sourdough and whole wheat)
- 8-inch whole wheat tortillas and corn tortillas

Fish

- 2 (15-ounce) cans of water-packed tuna
- 2 cans of minced clams
- 2 cans of anchovies

Wine and Sherry

- 1 bottle each of good dry red wine, dry white wine, and port
- 1 bottle of dry sherry
- Marsala wine

Baking Needs

- All-purpose flour
- Cake flour
- Baking soda
- Baking powder
- Powdered sugar
- Sugar
- Brown sugar
- Honey
- 1 pound each raw almonds, walnuts, and pecans
- Raisins
- 2 bags of semisweet chocolate chips
- 1 (9-ounce) bar each of semisweet, unsweetened, and bittersweet chocolate

MUST-HAVE STAPLE ITEMS

Even though some of these staples don't have a long shelf life, they'll stay fresh between trips to the market and inspire delicious meals every day of the week.

Fruits
+ 6 lemons
+ 6 limes

Vegetables
+ 6 yellow onions
+ 4 white onions
+ 1 red onion
+ 2 bunches of scallions (there are usually 8 to 10 scallions in a bunch)
+ 4 shallots
+ 2 garlic bulbs
+ 1 bunch of celery
+ 2 heads of romaine lettuce or your favorite lettuce
+ 2 tomatoes
+ 2 avocados
+ Assorted vegetables, such as zucchini, cucumbers, and broccoli

+ 1 bag of carrots (at least 12 carrots)
+ 1 (1-pound) bag of frozen peas
+ 1 (1-pound) bag of frozen spinach

Herbs
+ 1 bunch of Italian parsley
+ 1 bunch of fresh basil

Dairy
+ 1 dozen cage-free organic eggs
+ 1 pound (4 sticks) unsalted butter
+ 1 (8-ounce) package each of cream cheese and low-fat or nonfat cream cheese
+ 8 ounces of Monterey jack and sharp cheddar cheese
+ 6 to 8 ounces of feta cheese
+ 6 to 8 ounces of goat cheese
+ Sour cream
+ 1 quart buttermilk
+ 1 pint half-and-half
+ 1 quart each of low-fat and nonfat milk

Meat
+ Roasted chicken from the market

Spices
+ 1 box of kosher salt
+ 1 box of table salt
+ Black peppercorns
+ Red pepper flakes
+ Cayenne pepper
+ Garlic powder
+ Onion powder
+ Whole nutmeg
+ Chili
+ Ancho chili powder
+ Cumin
+ Coriander
+ Curry
+ Hungarian paprika
+ Dry mustard
+ Saffron
+ Dried oregano, rosemary, and thyme
+ Caraway seeds
+ Fennel seeds
+ Bay leaves
+ Ground ginger
+ Ground cloves
+ Vanilla extract
+ Ground cinnamon
+ Arrowroot
+ Cornstarch
+ Sesame seeds

ACKNOWLEDGMENTS

To God, who speaks to me every day. I can hear Him clearly when I stop, get quiet, and actually listen to what He is telling me.

My husband, Tony, is my soul mate and the most important person in my life. We have shared twenty-five years of crazy love, family, food, and working side by side with one goal, the strength of our family unit and devotion to each other. I'm crazy hyper; he is not. He's grounded, centered, and beautiful. He gives me wings, watches me fly, and catches me when I fall.

To my mother, who devoted all of her life to her family and instilled in me, my sister, Diana, and my brother, Gino, the importance of love, giving back, loyalty, tradition, and keeping the family unit strong!

My daughters, Kathryn, Alexandra, and Arianna, are my reason for everything I do in my life. They are my joy and passion; just thinking of them fills my soul. Seeing or speaking with them is the happiest part of my day. The world stops when they call or come over.

To my stepchildren, Anne, Denis, and Mark, whose love and respect I work hard at because of my enormous love and respect for them. They are in every fiber of my heart and soul, and our family is one.

To my grandchildren, Claire, Kevin, Acacia, and Seraphina. Wow—who knew the added bonus that grandkids bring! I actually love them so unconditionally that they can do pretty much what they want and all I do is laugh, then give them hugs and too many kisses. They think I'm the best thing that has ever happened to them. I love them more than anything. They bring nothing but pure joy into my life. We cook and bake together, and they love everything I cook for them, and so . . . we continue on with tradition.

Jan Miller has been my literary agent and best friend for many years. I love her deeply, like a sister. I don't know anyone like her. She is my mentor, and if I had to pick the one person I would most like to be like, it would be her. She inspires me and constantly amazes me with her boundless energy in every aspect of her life, especially when it comes to helping others. She is full of fiery passion and is fiercely (and I don't use that term lightly) loyal, a razor-sharp businessperson, enormously fun and funny, and compassionate to a fault. No one makes me laugh like she does. She keeps me on my toes. She knew how much this book meant to me and made it happen, and I am so grateful to her.

Pat Moller is my soul-connection girlfriend who thinks exactly like I do. All we do is eat and laugh all the time. It doesn't stop! I talk to her every day. She is my rock, and what I really like the most (no, I don't) is that she tells it to me like it really is. She doesn't sugarcoat anything and is brutally honest with me about everything. Pat and her husband, Finn (my pal too), were the guinea pigs for this book. They taste tested every single recipe in this book, and if it got past them, it made it into the pages of this book.

Annie Gilbar, my cherished friend, is my go-to person, whom I dubbed the Wise One. She is there when I need grounding, counsel, encouragement, hugs, and spell checks. A brilliant writer and editor, she helps me make sense of it all, even my life. She and her husband, Gary, are at our home often, and they taste test my food, even though all Annie ever wants to eat is angel hair pasta. We sit for hours over a meal and talk and talk and talk. Annie looks over my writing, is a mentor to my girls, and helps me personally in so many ways. She is my safe place. Fanny, we are forever!

Amy and Andy Heyward are our extended family. Every Sunday is movie night at the Heywards'. Amy always has a beautiful smile on her face; she's full of life, extremely generous, kind, loving, and supportive; and she's a load of fun to be with. We laugh a lot when we are together. We "get" each other and have a special heart connection. Amy is a vegetarian and makes unbelievable vegetarian food; she has shown me how to make some incredible dishes that have helped me shape a lot of the ways I cook and prepare veggies. Andy is like a brother to my Tony; he is also one of my guinea pigs, taste testing a lot of the recipes for this book. I love him, but he won't eat anything green even though he's married to a vegetarian! We share our lives together with food, family, friends, and lots of love. "LUMI."

Suzy Unger, my dear friend, literally swooped into my life almost two years ago and attacked me in an exercise class demanding to know why I wasn't back on TV doing a show. She was an agent at the William Morris Agency at the time, and in a matter of a few months I was back on the air. She is a tender, good-hearted, and loving person who is always there for me and my family. My girls love and adore Suzy and consider her their girlfriend. She has been and is a true blessing in my life, and I will hold on to her always.

A very special thank you to the Lerios family—Cory, Maria, Andrew, Michael, and Demitri—for their hospitality, support, and generosity. They brought so much joy, love, music, and laughter into our life and home. We tested a lot of recipes for this book with them and had so much fun doing it! I love and adore each and every one of them with all my heart. Thank you for opening up your beautiful home to us and helping me with this book.

Sid and Cheryl Tessler are the foundation on which our family stands. Knowing that Sid and Cheryl are there keeps our whole family feeling grounded and safe. Sid and Tony are the best of friends and love each other deeply. I hang my hat on that, knowing that they are there and no matter what life throws at us we will be fine.

My sweet Marina Ponce has been our family backbone for eighteen years. I don't think I would have been able to finish this book on time if it weren't for her tireless effort in keeping my life and all the chaos in the kitchen in check as we prepared all of dishes and photographed them here in our home. You are a blessing to us all.

Diane Cu and Todd Porter took the amazing photos for this book. It was as if a special force brought us together somehow. The whole experience working with them was magical and effortless, even though we had the monumental task of getting more than two hundred photos finished in a very short time. I fell in love with the both of them on day one. Their passion for life, food, and each other is inspiring. Their kindness, patience, and generosity are overwhelming! Sometimes you get an unexpected gift in life that elevates you to a new place. Thank you, Diane and Todd—I can't wait to do it again!

Thank you, Michael Fragnito, for being my champion on this project. I knew the instant that we met that Sterling was to be my new home. We made a connection, and you made this happen. This book is a true labor of love and means so much to me. It has been wrapped up in my head for so long, and this is a dream come true. I am so grateful to you for going to bat for me, and I am so grateful to have had the opportunity to meet and work with you and everyone I have met at Sterling.

Jennifer Williams, usually editors scare me, but you are so amazing—all I wanted to do was make you happy! You are extremely kind, patient, and nurturing. This was a huge undertaking given the time frame we were given. I panicked; you did not. You helped keep me centered and focused and made me feel like I could deliver. That helped me keep my eye on the ball because all I wanted to do was make you proud. Thank you for your tireless effort in delivering this book.

Chris Thompson, I couldn't wait every day to get the photos back to you for your input. I was so proud of them, and I knew you would work your magic. Thank you for your patience and kindness during a couple of meltdowns when I thought the world was coming to an end, when you ever so politely suggested that I try a couple of things another way. You were right, and the book is deliciously beautiful. Thank you for all your help!

Eileen Chetti, thank you for pulling this book together in no time and making sense of it all. I've learned so much from you, and I'm in awe at your extraordinary talent in helping organize the recipes to make this book so user-friendly. You brought it to life. Thank you so much!

My daughter Alex Thomopoulos was my sous-chef and right hand, literally, during the photo shoot of the food. This was the most difficult but the most fun part of doing this book. She kept everything organized and the kitchen running smoothly. You were amazing, Alex, and I could not have done this without your help. Thank you. "I'm bursting."

I look at my life in chapters, and this is definitely my "Dream-Come-True Chapter." This book and my cooking show, *Cristina Ferrare's Big Bowl of Love*, would not have happened without the blessings and support of Oprah Winfrey. Thank you, Oprah. I am deeply grateful. It's been so exciting to be a small part in this newest chapter of your life. Yours has definitely been a page-turner, with much more to come.

Special Thank-you

I take great pride in our home, and I'm so particular and passionate about the look and feel, especially when it comes to eating and entertaining. It's important to me that everyone who comes over feels welcomed and comfortable. What I choose to decorate my tables with and serve my food on is something I give a lot of thought to. As I've stated in the book, "I believe people eat with their eyes first." Not only does the food have to excite, tantalize, and taste delicious, but also what you serve it in and how you present it is just as important. It makes the whole dining experience enjoyable and fun, no matter if it's a sandwich or big beautiful bowl of pasta.

I want to thank the following people and companies whose merchandise I collect, love, and use. They were kind enough to lend me more pieces for this book. My food looks amazing; just look at the pieces they are served in!

Brian Thorson and Tim Hosier (ferrarewithcompany.com/)
Lee Feldman, MacKenzie Childs (www.MacKenzie-childs.com/official)
Elad Yifrach, L'Objet (l-objet.com)
John Hardy, Vagabond House (www.vagabondhouse.com)
Diane Seidle, Mustardseed & Moonshine (www.mustardseedandmoonshine.com)

INDEX

Note: Page numbers in **bold** indicate recipe category lists.